# FUSIONS: INTEGRATING VALUES IN ONLINE EDUCATION

Jane M. Govoni
Mary T. Spoto
Valerie Wright

*Saint Leo University*

**KENDALL/HUNT PUBLISHING COMPANY**
4050 Westmark Drive    Dubuque, Iowa 52002

# CONTENTS

# PREFACE

The impetus for this book is to address the current focus on values in online education and to provide a text that offers learning opportunities for the integration of values across disciplines and learning venues. It is intended to bring awareness and understanding of how integral values are to the academic, professional, and personal life of an individual. Recognizing the life altering force of values, the authors intend the book to serve students at all stages of their journey toward a values-infused life.

The authors wanted to make this topic of values integration across the curriculum amenable to both online learners and professor alike. The readers will find:

1. The book is written for the online student. The tone and content are tailored to the interest of the student, making every effort to engage on the student's level. In striving to make a match that works, the authors piloted various chapters during a focus group of traditional and non-traditional age university students from different majors and academic levels.

2. The book is written for instructors bearing in mind their differing levels of experience in presenting this topic, their familiarity with this topic, and their desires for flexible activities that can be easily included in discussions. Toward these ends, the authors organized the activities according to value and then discipline, providing suggestions on how to deliver these activities in a classroom setting.

The aim of **Part I** is to acquaint the reader with various facets of values education. It begins with a brief personal inventory; it is suggested that the reader complete the inventory before moving to the other sections of the book. The chapter continues with an historical overview of one university and its Benedictine heritage. To keep things interesting, the authors have included some little known facts about the history of the university in a series of vignettes entitled *History or Hearsay*. Look for these and an historical timeline of the university! Part I ends with a focus on student life in an online environment. The reader will have an opportunity to try out numerous activities relating online learning to values.

**Part I** includes a focus on values in and after academia and the importance of values on the reader's professional and personal life after graduation. Chapter 2 contains an overview of the development and trends in values education, defining the approach one university has adopted for its students, and ends with reflections on how values can shape and affect life for the better after graduation. The reader will also enjoy a photo gallery of pictures of Saint Leo University's past and present that separates Parts I and II.

**Part II** begins the activities section of the book. Here, the reader will find a series of practical activities designed for the online classroom and organized according to a select core of Benedictine inspired values. Yet while part of a long Benedictine tradition, these values are universal in nature and adopted by people of differing cultures and backgrounds. These values are excellence, community, respect, personal development, responsible stewardship, and integrity.

The organization of **Part II** affords both faculty and online learners alike a chance to choose how they want to use this book. Readers can look for a value they are interested in and learn how different disciplines might implement that particular value. Conversely, if readers want to know how a particular discipline implements multiple values, they can look at the *Outline of Values by Discipline* found in the Appendix.

Overall, the activities in **Part II** are varied enough to use in multiple ways. Instructors may use an activity as a discussion, leading to more sustained and reflective discussion, or they may opt to use a variety of activities to give students multiple perspectives. No activity alone can teach values, for values are complex and rich. But in the end, the authors hope this book engenders lively discussion and thoughtful reflection and leads readers to further explore values as part of academics and in society, the community, and the individual's life.

Cindy Lee, Ph.D.

# AUTHORS' ACKNOWLEDGMENTS

We would like to extend a sincere thank you to the entire university community for their time, patience, commitment, and support in assisting us throughout this process. It has been such a wonderful experience and we believe that our tireless efforts in creating exemplar activities for 'students' to gain the true essence of a values curriculum are well presented in this book.

We also extend a special thanks to our families and friends who supported our endeavors.


Jane, Mary, and Valerie
Saint Leo University

# MEET THE CONTRIBUTING EDITORS

Astolfi, Douglas, M., Vice President for Academic Affairs, Saint Leo University
Conway, Jody, Assistant Director, Center for Online Learning, Saint Leo University
Criss, Robert (Randy), Associate Professor, Physics, Saint Leo University
Cronin, Christopher, Chair, Psychology, Saint Leo University
Dadez, Edward W., Vice President for Student Affairs, Saint Leo University
Kieffer, Kevin, Assistant Professor, Psychology, Saint Leo University
Krogol, Jude, O.S.B., Saint Leo Abbey
Lee, Cindy, Associate Professor, Social Work, Saint Leo University
MacEachran, Joanne, Director of Academic Student Support Services, Saint Leo University
Moon, Carol Ann, Reference Librarian and Assistant Professor, Saint Leo University
Noe, Sasha N., Assistant Director, Center for Online Learning, Saint Leo University
Pierce, Anne, Adjunct, Virginia Center, Saint Leo University
Robles, Magda, Circulation Supervisor, Saint Leo University
Schoultz, Carolyn, Assistant Professor, Education, Saint Leo University
Stier, Mark M., Director for Residence Life and Judicial Coordinator, Saint Leo University
Thomas, Rebekah, Associate Professor, Science, University of Texas Corpus Christi
White, Jacquelyn A. (Jacci), Associate Professor, Mathematics, Saint Leo University

*A very special thank you is extended to **Siobhan Herkert,** a senior in the Elementary Education Department, for her creativity, patience, and willingness to share her artistic talents. Siobhan drew the illustrations throughout the text.*

*A special thanks to **Carol Ann Moon,** Reference Librarian, for searching for quotes on values to match each discipline.*

*A special thanks to **Sister Dorothy Neuhofer, O.S.B.,** Director of Library Services and Archivist, for sharing so much of Saint Leo's history.*

*A special thank you to **Doris Van Kampen,** Assistant Professor, Systems Librarian, for her willingness and extended time in scanning the historical pictures of Saint Leo.*

*Another special thanks to **Lorrie Zelakowski,** a senior in the Elementary Education Department for her photos of the present day Saint Leo campus.*

# MEET THE SUPPORT PEOPLE

A special thanks is extended to the following individuals for their time and support with stories, ideas, activities, quotes, editing, and reviews:

Bagley, Ann, Chair, Education Department
Cooper, Michael, S.J., Assistant to the President for Campus Ministry
Crosby, Thomas (Tim), Associate Professor of Physical Education, Head Tennis Coach
Durst, Maribeth, Dean, School of Education and Social Services
Fox, Liana, Ph.D. Mathematics, Tampa Florida
Kirk, Arthur, F., Jr., President of Saint Leo University
Kissel, Anthony, S.T.D., Associate Professor, Religious Studies
Koval, Calista, Associate Professor, Education
Lee, Allan, Senior Pastor, Nassau, Bahamas
Mallue, Marilyn M., Professor, Psychology, Virginia Center
Moore, Daniel, Coordinator, Psychology Program, Brevard College
Moorman, Michael, Chair, Business Administration
Noe, Sasha, Assistant Director, Center for Online Learning
Pacella III, Father Michael, Vicar, Adjunct, South Hampton Roads Center, Virginia
Sing, William, Student Assistant and Senior, Business
Trost, Jennifer A., Assistant Professor, History
Urban Impact Ministries, Discipleship Team, New Orleans, Louisiana
Van Wilt, Kurt, Associate Professor, English

> Watch your thoughts; they become words.
>
> Watch your words; they become actions.
>
> Watch your actions; they become habits.
>
> Watch your habits; they become character.
>
> Watch your character; it becomes your destiny.
>
> —*Frank Law*

> Evaluation and judgment are responses to what exist, sorting the things that pass before us into categories of good, bad, and indifferent. But a rational life, the life of a valuer, does not consist essentially in reaction. It consists in action . . .
>
> —*David Kelly*

**fusion**   (fyoo'zhen) n. 1. the merging of different elements into a union. 2. the state of fact of being so united. 3. joining together.

People write books for many reasons. Some write to entertain, others to unveil hidden truths, others to instruct, and still others to holistically document. In the case of this book, the purpose was really very simple: to help you understand what a values-centered education is all about and to give you opportunities to actively engage in thinking about how values inform, deepen, and distinguish your online learning. In this way, we have chosen the word **fusion** to give you a picture of how various disciplines may all unite in this pursuit, demonstrating how the question of values may affect how you chat online, how you conduct research, how you view history, or even how you post your writings.

As you move through the text, you will discover the thoughts and theories behind values education which have influenced programs of study in colleges and universities throughout the U.S. We'll also travel back in time to see the history of one university and its dedication and hard work of the founding Benedictine monks and sisters who laid the foundations for the values-inspired culture that is enjoyed at this university. Then it will be time to actively engage in activities, which will give you an opportunity to put the values to your own individual test. Your instructors may choose activities to integrate in your online education experiences. You may find yourself focusing on excellence in math, integrity in English class, or responsible stewardship in sociology. We encourage you also to try some of these activities for yourself as well. Revisit them. Compare your notes. How does the value of respect influence your study of social groups, of people of various ages, races, or economic classes? How does this same value affect the way your colleague studies science? You may discover subjects that once seemed separate and distant from each other are not so very different after all. In fact, they may fuse into a greater whole—a body of knowledge working in harmony that can guide and inspire you to think, to act, and to lead a more fulfilling and successful life.

# PART I

# ACADEMIC AND SOCIAL CULTURES FOR ONLINE LEARNERS

# CHAPTER 1

# PERSPECTIVES

# FROM ONE UNIVERSITY

**Pssst . . .**

Check out the textboxes throughout Chapters 1 and 2— **Is it history or hearsay?** and *Saint Leo Firsts!*

At Saint Leo University, educating you as a student means giving you the tools to awaken your highest potential, to recognize the importance of values in your life, and to empower you with the knowledge that you need *not* "take the world as it comes" but to use a values-defined education to change the world— and yourself—for the better. In designing a program to provide you with extensive, multiple opportunities for intellectual development and discovery, the university identified the following six core values central to the education of mind, body, and spirit: excellence, community, respect, personal development, responsible stewardship, and integrity. One or more of these values are emphasized in your online courses. The values are universal. You have the opportunity to learn to understand, judge, and live these values based on your commitment to your studies and personal goals. Ultimately, we hope that you will share with us how these values have influenced your personal and professional lives.

**August 10, 1881**
*Edward F. Dunne granted land for Catholic Colony in Florida.*

**February 1, 1886**
*Bishop John Moore requested from Benedictine Archabbot Boniface Wimmer assistance in developing a Benedictine community.*

**May 12, 1886**
*Fr. Gerard Pilz arrived to develop Benedictine college.*

**October 10, 1888**
*Saint Vincent Archabbey in Pennsylvania transferred Benedictine jurisdiction to Maryhelp Abbey in North Carolina.*

Reflection Activity

### *Where Are You Now?*

Let's find out where you are now in interpreting these core values by completing the following questionnaire.

Name: _____     Date: _____

Freshman     Sophomore     Junior     Senior     Transfer

On Campus     Online

Major: _____

1. Briefly define each of the core values in your own words.

    Excellence
    Community
    Respect
    Personal Development
    Responsible Stewardship
    Integrity

2. Choose *three* of the core values that you feel are most important for a "citizen" in today's society. Place a check next to these values.

    _____ Excellence
    _____ Community
    _____ Respect
    _____ Personal Development
    _____ Responsible Stewardship
    _____ Integrity

3. Which value do you place more emphasis on in your *daily life?* Why?


4. Which value will *most likely* be emphasized in your *future career?* Why?

Keep your responses in this book and sometime during your last semester at your university, re-take this questionnaire to reflect on your personal growth. Keep one other point in mind, too. A values-inspired academic life informs everything you do, from how you interact online to how you study for an exam. So, let's turn our attention to study skills to reflect briefly on your habits. Harvard professor Richard Light reports "The college years are a time of change, introspection, questioning, exploration of what a student believes in . . ." (167).

| **February 7, 1889** | **February 28, 1889** | **June 4, 1889** | **July 1889** |
|---|---|---|---|
| *Abbot Leo Haid, O.S.B. of Maryhelp Abbey accepted a gift of 36 acres of Lake Jovita from Judge Dunne.* | *The Benedictine sisters of Holy Name Convent arrived from Allegheny, Pennsylvania.* | *Date Saint Leo College and Abbey were founded.* | *Mother Dolorosa Scanlon, O.S.B. became prioress.* |

### *Me, Myself, and I*

Read the statements below and check the ones you feel are applicable to you.

\_\_\_\_ I sometimes feel isolated.

\_\_\_\_ I usually hesitate to ask for help.

\_\_\_\_ I do not organize my time well.

\_\_\_\_ I organize my college studying just like I did in high school.

\_\_\_\_ I find it difficult to change my study habits.

\_\_\_\_ I am not sure how to select my courses.

\_\_\_\_ I usually study alone.

*Source: Light, Richard (2001).*

Light's interviews lead him to conclude that struggling college students would check off *all* of the above statements. At your university you are surrounded with opportunities to learn about yourself while building on your intellectual development. This book provides you with a wealth of opportunities to help you improve your study habits through connections made with the six core values. You will be presented with a variety of activities based on these values to complete on your own, or as assigned by your instructors. You will be asked to share your thoughts, defend your rationale, and/or reflect on your college experiences and future endeavors. However, prior to engaging in these values-based activities, take time to read about Saint Leo's fascinating history and its Benedictine heritage. You will see how one university lived the values to impact not only the educational lives of its students but also the greater community.

## AN HISTORICAL OVERVIEW

In the early 1880s, Judge Edmund Francis Dunne, ex-chief Justice of Arizona, was instrumental in developing the San Antonio colony in Pasco County, Florida. Today these boundaries consist of San Antonio, St. Joseph, and St. Leo. A reverent believer in Catholic education, he was granted thousands of acres of land for the development of a Catholic colony from Hamilton Disston, a 37-year-old entrepreneur who had purchased 4 million acres of land from the state of Florida. Our longtime history professor, James Horgan, masterfully describes this evolution in his book *Pioneer College: The Centennial History of Saint Leo College, Saint Leo Abbey, and the Holy Name Priory.* Horgan records Dunne's 1885 commentary to a reporter for the *Baltimore Catholic Mirror* as follows:

**Is it history or hearsay?**

Spirits of the Benedictine monks buried in the Grotto still haunt the main campus grounds at night.

*Although our first reaction is to deny the thought of seeing or hearing any ghosts,* two freshmen walked through the Grotto late one evening in October 2003 and claimed to have heard footsteps behind them. So, what is definitely history is that Father Mohr, the first abbot of Saint Leo, is buried in the Grotto.

**August 19, 1890**

Saint Leo's first abbot, Father Charles Mohr inaugurated as leader of the military college.

**September 13, 1890**

James L. McDermott, Jr., first student of Saint Leo College, arrived by train from Key West.

**October 7, 1890**

College library established.

**December 28, 1891**

Death of first Saint Leo student, Conrad Metzner, who was accidentally shot during a military drill.

## Is it history or hearsay?

In 1917, the monks of Saint Leo Abbey were dubbed the "murderous monks of Pasco County."

***It's history AND hearsay.*** An anti-Catholic politician named Tom Watson of Georgia did indeed coin the term the "murderous monks of Pasco County." However, the inflammatory phrase was the product of anti-Catholic sentiment rather than real-life drama. In 1916, the death of a candidate running for tax assessor brewed wild rumors that members of Catholic organizations murdered him because his platform included taxing church property, thus giving Catholics the motive for murder. During the same period, Watson continued his attacks on the monks by issuing a statement that they might assassinate Sydney J. Catts, who was running for governor on an openly anti-Catholic platform.

> I obtained . . . the right to have the first selection [of land], out of the purchase 50,000 acres of land for a Catholic colony, with the privilege that when I had sold a certain amount I should have the further privilege of taking another 50,000 acres for the same purpose. This contract was made August 10, 1881. On August 19, I was in Florida and began the work of this section.

Dunne had purposefully named the colony "San Antonio" after the patron, Saint Anthony, to whom he prayed for assistance while looking for lost silver in the Arizona desert years ago. His arrival in San Antonio on Saint Jovita's Day on February 15, 1882 gave way to the naming of Lake Jovita, earlier known as Clear Lake.

Four years later, Judge Dunne spoke with Bishop John Moore of Saint Augustine regarding the possibility of a monastery and with this began the history of Saint Leo. Bishop John Moore petitioned Archabbot Boniface Wimmer of St. Vincent Archabbey in Latrobe, Pennsylvania for assistance from the Benedictines to develop Saint Leo College, its abbey, and the Holy Name Priory.

> San Antonio, Hernando County, Florida
> February 1, 1886
>
> Rt. Rev. Archabbot Wimmer, O.S.B.,
> St. Vincent Abbey
>
> Rt. Rev. Abbot,
>
> I have here a mission which I believe could be directed by our Fathers with the greatest advantage to the colonists and one also which I am confident would be a source of much consolation to the priests who would take charge of it. There are here now about four hundred Catholics, the majority of whom

**September 11, 1892**

*Official U.S. Weather Bureau Station established at Saint Leo.*

**April 2, 1894**

*The cupola of the main college building was removed when tourists requested tours by the monks to view the rolling hills and countryside.*

**September 29, 1894**

*Mrs. James Mooney, Saint Leo's first woman teacher hired.*

**January 6, 1895**

*Youngest student arrived, Jesus M. Fernandez, son of the Cuban vice consul in Tampa, at age seven.*

are Germans. Other families are expected to arrive soon. If you are willing to assume the charge of this mission I would suggest that you send down here a father who knows the German and English languages and who would take full cognizance of all things here and report to you. I empower you to give the faculties of the priests of this diocese to any father whom you may elect to send on the mission. Judge Dunne, the founder of this colony, has a valuable tract of land in reserve, especially kept over for the Benedictine Fathers if only they are willing to come here and accept this offer and the charge of the mission. As far as I can judge there is here a fine field for missionary labor, and one for which your fathers are especially adapted.

I am on my way to Key West and Havana, and if you should honor me with a reply I will request that you direct your letter to me in Key West, in care of the Rev. Father Ghione.

If you should decide to send a father here he can come by rail to Dade City, which is only six miles distant from the town of San Antonio. On arriving at Jacksonville he should take the Tampa and Key West railroad to the Palatka Junction and come down here on the Florida Southern railroad. At Dade City there is a livery stable where he can get a conveyance to take him to San Antonio.

Hoping, Rt. Rev. Abbot, that you will be able to accept the charge of this mission and asking your prayers, I am,

Yours truly in Christ,
John Moore, D.D.
Bishop of St. Augustine

Letter to Rt. Rev. Abbot, February 1, 1886 from Saint Vincent Archabbey Archives

**Is it history or hearsay?**

Pope Saint Leo the Great reigned during the invasion of Attila the Hun. According to the perhaps apocryphal story when Attila marched on Rome, Pope Saint Leo the Great went out to meet him, pleading with him to leave. Legend holds that Attila saw the vision of a man in priestly robes, carrying a bare sword and threatening to kill the invader if he did not obey, and Attila turned away from the gates of the eternal city.

*Perhaps it is a little of both history and hearsay.* Some writers reported that Attila's vision was of Saint Peter, the visionary opponent to the Huns. Rome was saved and the Huns banished.

| **July 1895** | **December 1, 1896** | **July 1898** | **March 25, 1906** |
|---|---|---|---|
| *Mother Boniface Feldman, O.S.B. became prioress.* | *Dr. Gatton of San Antonio traded one gallon of milk daily in payment for his son's tuition.* | *Mother Rose Marie Easly, O.S.B. became prioress.* | *The cornerstone laid for Saint Leo Abbey.* |

## EARLY LEADERS IN ESTABLISHING AND DEVELOPING SAINT LEO

*Judge Edmond Dunne*

*Bishop John Moore, Saint Augustine*

*Archabbot Boniface Wimmer of St. Vincent Archabbey, Pennsylvania*

*Rev. Gerald Pilz, pioneer Benedictine in Florida*

*Bishop Leo Haid of Maryhelp Abbey, North Carolina*

*Rev. Charles Mohr, Director of Saint Leo College at 30 years of age and 40 years of age*

*Rev. Benedict Roth, pioneer monk and archivist*

Judge Edmund F. Dunne as he appeared in *McGee Illustrated Weekly,* February 10, 1877 from the Edward J. Herrmann Collection; Archabbot Boniface Wimmer and Rev. Gerald Pilz from Saint Vincent Archabbey Archives; all others from Saint Leo Abbey Archives.

Archabbot Wimmer, from the Order of Saint Benedict (O.S.B.), accepted and in the spring of 1886 Rev. Gerald Pilz, O.S.B. was sent to San Antonio to oversee the mission. Pilz spoke both German and English and initiated the proposal for a Benedictine College. However, as you can imagine, supporting a community from such a far distance as Pennsylvania was too cumbersome. So, in 1888, Archabbot Wimmer transferred the jurisdiction of the Florida mission to the Benedictines of Maryhelp Abbey in Belmont, North Carolina (now Belmont Abbey College). It was Abbot-Bishop Leo Haid of Maryhelp Abbey who founded Saint Leo College and the Saint Leo Abbey on June 4, 1889. As founder, he was one of three inspirational figures for whom the Abbey and the College were named. The other two were Pope Saint Leo the Great (440–461) and Pope Leo XIII, who reigned at the time of the college's establishment. Horgan reports that Bishop Leo Haid was "the principal Leo for whom the college is named" (85).

**Summer 1910**

*Saint Leo colors changed to purple and gold.*

**July 5, 1911**

*The Holy Name Convent and Academy building was transported by oxen from its original site in San Antonio to the current site of the Holy Name Monastery.*

**March 27, 1916**

*Mr. Henry Moeller, or Handsome Henry as he was called, began working on the Grotto of Lourdes.*

**June 5, 1917**

*Six Saint Leo clerics and brothers registered for military draft. Close to 100 Saint Leo men served in the armed forces during World War I.*

*The three Leos for whom Saint Leo is named*
The three Leo's from Saint Leo Abbey and Belmont Abbey Archives

As these first Benedictine monks began their work, Father Gerald Pilz petitioned a group of Benedictine sisters from Allegheny, Pennsylvania to the town of San Antonio to begin an elementary school for girls. A group of five sisters, led by Sister Dolorosa Scanlon, arrived in February 1889, and immediately began organizing a school and creating a presence in the community whose spiritual influence continues to this day.

**Is it history or hearsay?**

Father Charles Mohr, O.S.B., first director of Saint Leo, had numerous Saint Bernard dogs; each one called "Fritz."

***It's history.*** Rev. Mohr was a great animal lover who had six Saint Bernards and one German shepherd all named Fritz. The final "Fritz" outlived his master, who died in 1924. The local newspaper reported, "It is impossible to properly estimate the good that is growing out of the work done by Father Charles and his able corps of assistants in promoting the social, moral, and educational refinement of our county. Saint Leo College takes rank with the very best institutions of learning in the South" (Pasco County Democrat, 1892).

*Charles Mohr in 1917*
From Saint Leo Abbey Archives

*Founding Benedictine Sisters in 1892*

*Front: Mother Dolorosa Scanlan, Sr. Boniface Feldmann*

*Back: Sr. Rose Marie Easly, Sr. Agatha Giesler, Sr. Immaculate Walters*

From Holy Name Priory Archives

**September 1920**

*Holy Name sisters opened boarding school for boys ages 5–12 called Saint Benedict's Preparatory School.*

**October 17, 1920**

*Holy Name Academy girls enrolled in science classes at Saint Leo.*

**July 1921**

*Mother Immaculate Walters, O.S.B. became prioress.*

**July 1924**

*Mother Rose Marie Easly, O.S.B. became prioress once again.*

In the 1890s, Rev. Charles Mohr announced to the students of Saint Leo Military School: "We think Christmas vacation is a nuisance, and hence will grant none."

***It's history.*** Rev. Mohr, chief operating officer for the school, had also decreed that extra vacation was "a great demoralizer" because students would forget what they had learned over vacation. Because of an influx of student petitions reacting to these statements, Rev. Mohr granted breaks for the holidays, perhaps beginning the Saint Leo tradition of being a learner-centered college.

Rev. Charles Mohr, the first director of Saint Leo, met with the President of the United States.

***It's history.*** On October 21, 1905 Rev. Charles Mohr was introduced to President Theodore Roosevelt in Jacksonville, Florida.

In 1890, at the age of 27, Rev. Charles H. Mohr, O.S.B., was appointed director and was influential in developing the Saint Leo Benedictine mission and its educational focus. He also served as postmaster and on the Benedictine Board of Trustees along with Bishop Leo Haid, Fathers Gerald Pilz, Roman Kirchner, and Benedict Roth. Both Fathers Mohr and Roth played pivotal roles in the development of Saint Leo. Father Roth preserved the chronological details of its history and was considered a pioneering monk for his work and efforts. He created the first college paper and was the Abbey printer for over 25 years. In the summer of 1890 he prepared for the arrival of the students.

*Founding Benedictine priests in 1888*
From Saint Leo Abbey Archives

It was on September 13th that the Orange Belt Railway train pulled into the San Antonio station carrying 12-year-old James Leonard McDermott Jr., from Key West, the first student at Saint Leo College. McDermott was a baseball player and active in the school play, but did not receive his Master of Accounts degree until 23 years later in 1913. At that time he was a partner of McDermott & Hanigan, Inc. Building Contractors in New York City. The other two students who arrived shortly after McDermott were Carleton E. Shelley from Palatka and John Spellman from Orlando. Shelley was also a baseball player and teammate of McDermott, secretary of the library association, member of the quartet, and received his Master of Accounts degree from Saint Leo. Spellman withdrew after one semester to return home to work and sadly died at the age of 21. In that first year, there were thirty-two students enrolled in the college class. Many events, some joyous and a few tragic, ushered in the beginnings of Saint Leo College. Many more surprising and inspirational events were to follow from the hiring of the first female teacher in 1894 to the great fire that destroyed the original monastery in 1928.

During its history, Saint Leo became a two-year military academy for boys, the majority of whom were from Central and South America. The Depression caused severe

**June 1, 1928**
*The original monastery burned to the ground.*

**April 3, 1931**
*Abbot Charles Mohr died at 68 and was buried in the Grotto.*

**Summer/Fall 1932**
*Camp Saint Leo opened for boys ages 8–16 and Father Marion Bowman appointed varsity coach/athletic director.*

**March 11, 1939**
*Two concrete lions arrived on campus.*

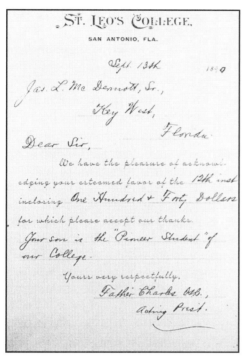

*First receipt issued by Saint Leo College*
From Saint Leo Abbey Archives

*James L. McDermott, Jr., pioneer student of Saint Leo College*
From Saint Leo Abbey Archives

**Is it history or hearsay?**

Saint Leo was a landmark area for tracking Floridian weather.

*It's history.* Brother Gerard Schneider kept weather records from 1857–1950, and the U.S. Weather Bureau called Saint Leo a "climatological benchmark" because of his thoroughness in weather records.

**Is it history or hearsay?**

Saint Leo received the nickname "the church that orange juice built."

*It's history.* The monks sent oranges and grapefruit from its citrus groves to Saint Meinrad Abbey of Indiana. In exchange, the Abbey supplied building materials. Some records indicate that the current student service building, DeChantal Hall, was used as an orange processing plant while others indicate the building where the Tavern is now located was the processing plant.

hardship on its continued development and by the early 1920s the college became a preparatory school for boys.

It was not until 1959 that Saint Leo again began to offer associate degrees and girls were admitted. So, for a short period of time Saint Leo was both a high school preparatory school and a college.

By the 1970s the college had 83 faculty members with a little over 1,000 students. Off-campus centers opened on military bases in the southeast and enrollment began to increase. New leadership came in the mid-1980s in the abbey, priory, and the college. In

*Saint Leo College in 1894*
From Saint Leo Abbey Archives

1987, Monsignor Mouch, the seventh college president reported, "Saint Leo College is the best kept secret in Florida" (Saint Leo College Magazine). Total enrollment including students on military bases was under 5,000 students.

Ten years later, in 1997, Arthur F. Kirk, Jr. became the eighth president of the college and in 1998 the mission statement was examined. Community members employed by the college conveyed their suggestions to a committee who then drafted a revised mission statement. A committee was also formed to identify values based on the institution's

**March 4, 1940**
*Academy Award winner Lee Marvin enrolled at Saint Leo College Preparatory School.*

**December 7, 1941**
*In the course of World War II, 14 Saint Leo graduates were killed in service.*

**November 30, 1944**
*Father Bede Gale designed a school coat of arms; 13 years later he designed the official seal for the college, its first logo.*

**January 6, 1945**
*Saint Leo gymnasium burned to the ground.*

Benedictine heritage and the mission statement. Of approximately eighteen core values identified, six were selected and defined.

In August 1999, the college became a university. This change reflected its strength in delivering a values-driven, liberal arts-based education in a global, technological, and competitive society. Three years later, the core values were appropriately matched to courses. Here are the definitions of each of the core values:

**Excellence**—Saint Leo University is an educational enterprise. All of us, individually and collectively, work hard to ensure that our students develop the character, learn the skills, and assimilate the knowledge essential to become morally responsible leaders. The success of our University depends upon a conscientious commitment to our mission, vision, and goals.

**Community**—Saint Leo University develops hospitable Christian learning communities everywhere we serve. We foster a spirit of belonging, unity, and interdependence based on mutual trust and respect to create socially responsible environments that challenge all of us to listen, to learn, to change, and to serve.

**Respect**—Animated in the spirit of Jesus Christ, we value all individuals' unique talents, respect their dignity, and strive to foster their commitment to excellence in our work. Our community's strength depends on the unity and diversity of our people, on the free exchange of ideas and on learning, living, and working harmoniously.

**Personal Development**—Saint Leo University stresses the development of every person's mind, spirit, and body for a balanced life. All members of the Saint Leo University community must demonstrate their commitment to personal development to help strengthen the character of our community.

*Is it history or hearsay?*

The Holy Name Convent and Academy was moved manually with the assistance of two oxen from its original location in San Antonio to its current location on campus.

*It's history.* On July 5, 1911, the three-story building was put on wooden rollers and moved from its original site north of San Antonio plaza to its current location a half-mile east of the Saint Leo campus by a crew of workers, two oxen, and a winch. An original piece of brick can still be seen at the home of the monastery's original location.

*Holy Name Convent and Academy, 1889*
From Saint Leo Abbey Archives

**September 1945**
*Campus radio station WLEO began broadcasting from Saint Edward Hall.*

**January 29, 1948**
*Saint Leo Abbey formally consecrated.*

**April 20, 1951**
*Construction began on Saint Francis Hall to honor retired Abbot Francis Sadlier.*

**June 30, 1954**
*Father Marion Bowman elected third abbot of Saint Leo College Preparatory School.*

**Responsible Stewardship**—Our Creator blesses us with an abundance of resources. We foster a spirit of service to employ our resources to university and community development. We must be resourceful. We must optimize and apply all of the resources of our community to fulfill Saint Leo University's mission and goals.

**Integrity**—The commitment of Saint Leo University to excellence demands that its members live its mission and deliver on its promise. The faculty, staff, and students pledge to be honest, just, and consistent in word.

*It is our goal in writing this book to provide you as an online learner with the opportunity to understand, discuss, and examine the core values that are central to the university's holistic approach to learning. It is one perspective from one university.*

## THE BENEDICTINE HERITAGE

Let's take a look at Saint Leo's educational philosophy, which is rooted in its Benedictine heritage founded in the Rule of Saint Benedict. This Rule is one of the oldest documents in the Western world that is still used today. It is helpful in looking at Saint Leo's past, present, and future. Saint Benedict is credited for writing the Rule in the fifth century as a guide in European monasteries. He used several sources from other saints and spiritual writers in his work. During these times of political upheavals and wars, Benedict escaped to the Apennine Mountains where he lived in a cave in Subiaco, a town about 30 miles east of Rome. He was later forced to leave Subiaco and traveled south to Cassino, a small town outside of Rome. It was in this Italian monastery where Saint Benedict wrote the Rule. *Now, you may be wondering, how a 1,500-year-old document relates to you as a Saint Leo student today?* It's simple, really. The Rule describes the basic values of Benedictine life and explains how these values are applicable to everyone. The wisdom of Benedict's Rule comes from its recognition of the importance of universal values. It is not truly a "rule" to control or demand something, but rather a way of life.

The Benedictine sisters of Holy Name Convent have gone through three name changes over the years.

*It's history.* The names have been Holy Name Convent and Academy, Holy Name Priory, and the current one, Holy Name Monastery.

The library used to be located in Saint Edward Hall.

*It's history.* In January 1927, Saint Edward Hall opened as a residence hall with semi-private rooms and accommodations for about 150 students. There was a "pop shop" on the third floor and the library was located on the first floor where the Trane Stop is presently located. Mandatory study halls were scheduled.

The Saint Leo Abbey Church was built with oranges over a 58-year period.

*It's history.* On January 29, 1948, Bishop Thomas McDonough formally consecrated the Saint Leo Abbey. It was partly built of sandstone trim obtained from Saint Meinrad Abbey, Indiana in trade for Saint Leo's oranges and grapefruits. The pioneer Benedictines used their resources to develop the school prior to the church.

**April 11, 1957**
*Groundbreaking for Saint Leo's library.*

**July 1958**
*Sister DeChantal Ducuing, O.S.B. became prioress.*

**1959**
*Construction of Holy Name Priory (now Holy Name Monastery).*

**January 1, 1959**
*Dr. John I. Leonard became the **first** president of Saint Leo College and served until his death in 1961.*

Reflection Activity

## Ways of Life

Carney Strange, Professor at Bowling Green State University, lists the following ways of life as central to the life of Saint Benedict in the Subiaco Abbey. Take a moment to review the list and check the ones you feel are important in your life today.

_____ Fairness

_____ Patience

_____ Integrity

_____ Discipline

_____ Moderation

_____ Forgiveness

_____ Truthfulness

_____ Daily prayer

_____ Spirit of peace

_____ Love of nature

_____ Community life

_____ Do every job well

_____ Concern for others

_____ Take a stand for justice

_____ Responsible stewardship

_____ Rootedness and belonging

_____ Treat everyone like Christ

_____ Value of each human being

_____ Respect for books and learning

_____ Education for the whole person

_____ Care and respect for the environment

_____ Obedience to and respect for authority

_____ A balanced life: prayer, work, relaxation

_____ Develop each person according to potential

_____ The importance of things is relative, not absolute.

*Source: Carney Strange, 2001*

**September 13, 1959**
*Saint Leo College admitted 61 males and six females for a four-year college program.*

**Fall 1959**
*College colors were changed to green and gold, after the abbey orange groves.*

**Spring 1961**
*Crawford Hall dedicated in honor of Father Vincent Crawford's grandfather, Senator George White Crawford, a four-term senator and Civil War veteran.*

**June 1961**
***Father Stephen Hermann, O.S.B.** became **second** college president and served until 1968.*

1. Rank order the top three items that are of most importance to you. E-mail your choices to your instructor.

Saint Leo University strives for an integrated education that encompasses the extensive and profound ideals of the Benedictines. To truly understand the Benedictine heritage, you may choose to read and re-read the Rule of Saint Benedict. It can be used as a guide for everyone. It is quite a basic and an individualistic Rule. In monasteries, the Rule directs the spiritual and daily living and provides time for "ora et labora, and lectio divina" (prayer and work, and spiritual reading). English Benedictine, Dom Knowles, shares, "Such are the main outlines of the life which Saint Benedict wished his monks to lead. A life of prayer, of meditative reading, and of work, lived in common under

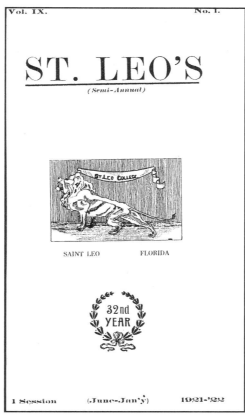

*Student newspaper*
From Saint Leo Abbey Archives

The Saint Leo newspaper has undergone numerous name changes over the years.

*One would probably surmise that this is true* given the historical changes that Saint Leo has undergone. The newspaper has been called *Saint Leo's Junior Spasms, The Chronicle, The Saint Leo Chronicle, The Saint Leo Chronicle-Reporter, The Lion, Monarch,* and *today it is called Lion's Pride.*

**March 4, 1962**
*Groundbreaking for McDonald Student Center.*

**May 22, 1964**
*Final commencement of Saint Leo College Preparatory School.*

**Spring 1964**
*Father Hermann initiated student service learning program that required each student to volunteer four hours per week in some campus capacity to foster the Benedictine spirit of community.*

**Spring, 1965**
*Holy Name Sisters began construction of Marmion Hall and Cafeteria and the Villa.*

one common father, and softened by a spirit of humanity which gave to all the daily relations the help of a natural and a supernatural affection" (16).

Overall, the Rule of Saint Benedict provides a foundational set of values with 21st-century relevance and is not just some parchment left behind in a dusty, ancient monastery. As one scholar puts it, "The Rule of Benedict is not concerned with a single time and place, a single view of church, a single set of devotions, or a single ministry. The Rule of Benedict is concerned with life: what it's about, what it demands, how to live it. And it has not failed a single generation" (Chittister, 19).

The Rule is written in less than one hundred pages; yet, as Sr. Dorothy Neuhofer, Director of the Saint Leo University library, sums it up, the Rule is "a literary classic and masterpiece of legislation." The Rule inspires spiritual and intellectual growth for leadership in the community, care for people, and respect for gifts and material items. In all, Saint Benedict shows a structured way of living with a sincere passion and provides flexibility as well as adaptability for change. The Rule gives shape to a common way of life today. Saint Benedict's purpose was not to institute a religious order but to set forth guidelines for daily living. Saint Benedict focuses on living in community. Your family is your first community and you have a community in college, church, workplace, and perhaps other places based on your lifestyle. It is in the community that you develop relationships and it is in relationships with others that you learn about yourself. In the Rule, you find a guide on how to overcome your shortcomings by working out your connectedness to others and yourself. You become more aware of how your decisions and your ways affect others as a whole. In summation, *you establish community values and strive for excellence.*

Is it history or hearsay?

Saint Leo alumni include several well-known actors.

**It's history.** Desi Arnaz, who played "Ricky" in *I Love Lucy* attended summer camp and Oscar-winning actor, Lee Marvin attended Saint Leo in the 1940s.

*Lee Marvin and Father Bowman in 1952*
From Saint Leo Abbey Archives

The **first** Catholic college in Florida was Saint Leo.

The **first** faculty member of the college was Father Benedict Roth, known as "pack rat" as he kept scrapbooks and chronologies of Saint Leo.

The **first** Holy Mass ever celebrated in Hernando and Pasco counties was offered at the home of Judge Edmond Dunne, where Saint Leo Abbey now stands.

The **first** teacher at Holy Name Academy was Sister Agnes Behe.

The **first** military uniforms for Saint Leo Military College arrived on January 10, 1891. They cost $13 and were grey with blue trim and a blue cap with "SLC" in gold. The uniform colors were a sign of reconciliation of the two opposing sides of the Civil War, Union blue and Confederate grey.

The **first** international student chosen to lead a company of cadets at Saint Leo College in 1891 was Jose Galindo of Havana, Cuba.

**April 4, 1965**
*Groundbreaking for girls dorm at Holy Name Priory (50 rooms for 100 women).*

**April 23, 1965**
*Saint Leo College incorporated as separate entity from Abbey.*

**Winter 1966**
*Holy Name Sisters began construction of Snyder Hall.*

**April 23, 1967**
*Fifty-one men and 13 women graduated from Saint Leo College.*

The **first** student to die at Saint Leo was Conrad Metzner, a candidate for priesthood. He was fatally shot when a rifle used for drilling practice went off accidentally on December 28, 1891.

The **first** "farm boss" was Brother Thomas Napiecek who planted orange groves.

The **first** performance on campus was presented on January 6, 1893. Pioneer student James McDermott introduced the show with these words: "This evening we will render a few dialogues and recitations for the first time in the history of the college. The entertainment is for your pleasure and we hope you will appreciate it. In the name of my colleagues I bid you a hearty welcome."

The **first** play was performed on May 3, 1893. It was called "A Public Benefactor" and was recorded as written by Brother Lawrence Wiegand, O.S.B., a popular young teacher. He died of tuberculosis four years later at the age of 23.

The **first** graduation at the college was for five students who received a degree of Master of Accounts on June 20, 1893: Oliver L. Arzacq, William T. McMurray, George C. Davis, J. Oscar Kennerly, and Carelton E. Shelly.

The **first** Saint Leo graduate to later earn a medical doctorate was Johannes Bodow, class valedictorian in 1894.

The **first** college colors were red, white, and blue (1896–97).

The **first** graduate of Holy Name Academy in 1897 was Bessie Bowen, daughter of former mayor of San Antonio.

The **first** Spanish-language Saint Leo catalogue was issued in 1898 called "El Colegio Militar de San León."

The **first** black student, Rudolph Antorcha, attended Saint Leo in 1899.

The **first** cold-water tap to student bathrooms was hooked up in 1900. Up to that point, the brother-housekeeper carried water and filled tubs.

The **first** foreign students enrolled at Saint Leo were from Cuba and Italy and in 1901–02 half of the student population was international.

The **first** telephone service began in 1903.

The **first** Saint Leo graduate to join the Benedictine community and become a priest was Aloysius Delabar in 1908.

The **first** automobile arrived at the Abbey in 1910.

The **first** student newspaper appeared in 1912. It was called *Saint Leo's* and sold for five cents. The paper was compiled in pamphlet form and included historical notes, stories on campus life, student jokes, and in its inaugural volume, a series of verses called "A Boy's Alphabet," with a stanza dedicated to a girl's name for each letter from "Anita" to "Zella."

**Is it history or hearsay?**

Saint Leo has had a "marching band" since the mid-1980s but no football team.

*It's history and hearsay.* A Saint Leo band had its first "gig" in the fall of 1984. It consisted of three Saint Leo students and two faculty members, but it was not a marching band. Today it is a seven-member band consisting of four faculty members. They play throughout the year for students and the community. They call themselves "Time Warp" and play to standing room only audiences in the community.

**Spring 1967**
*Julia Deal Lewis Hall constructed.*

**July 1, 1968**
*Anthony W. Zaitz, Saint Leo literature professor and chair of English department, became **third** president of college.*

**September 1968**
*Overall college enrollment peaked at 1,219.*

**March 27, 1969**
*College vested to Board of Trustees.*

The **first** electric lights were tested in Saint Leo Abbey and the **first** indoor plumbing was installed in college buildings in 1913.

The **first** literary magazine was published in 1919 called "The Saint Leo Cadet."

The **first** radio receiver was rigged by Fathers Paul Keegan and Philip Wartmann in 1921.

The **first** recorded interschool football game was in 1923 when Saint Leo was defeated by the Sacred Heart College Jesuit football team. The Lions played their **first** full regular schedule of football in 1924.

The **first** residence hall was Saint Edward Hall.

The **first** student resident in Saint Edward Hall was Marion Bowman in 1926. Many years later the Activities Center was named after him for his dedication to athletics and coaching.

The **first** issue of *The Lion* yearbook was published in 1929.

The **first** graduates of the first associate's degree class of Saint Leo College were conferred by President Father Stephen Hermann to 23 students in 1964.

The **first** P.E. major was Tim Crosby, current faculty member and head tennis coach.

The **first** bachelor's degree was conferred to 64 graduates who were members of the first four-year graduating class in 1967.

The **first** and only campus-wide demonstration occurred when students wanted women's visitation rights in the men's residence halls in the early 1970s.

The **first** athletic team as a four-year college was baseball.

The **first** Continuing Education Center opened in Virginia in 1974.

The **first** bachelor's degree conferred to full-time online student was in 2000.

The **first** wireless connection to the internet on university campus with Apple iBooks for faculty and students was in Fall 2001.

The **first** count for the Coalition for the Homeless of Pasco County by the Social Work Department at Saint Leo was in Fall 2001.

The **first** "state-of-the-art" residence halls opened on university campus in Fall 2003.

**May 1970**
*Marion Bowman Activities Center opened.*

**July 1, 1970**
*"Retired" **Abbot Bowman** served as **fourth** college president for one year.*

**July 1, 1971**
*Dr. Thomas Southard, former superintendent of schools for Pinellas County, Florida, became **fifth** college president and served until 1985.*

**July 1972**
*Sister Dorothy Neuhofer, O.S.B. became prioress.*

**Is it history or hearsay?**

Saint Leo has undergone numerous changes in its name. The last change was initiated by its eighth president.

***It's history.*** See the names and dates below. It was Dr. Arthur F. Kirk, Jr. who was instrumental in changing it from a college to a university.

| | |
|---|---|
| 1890 | St. Leo College |
| 1890–1903 | St. Leo Military College |
| 1903–1917 | St. Leo College |
| 1917–1918 | St. Leo College Preparatory School |
| 1918–1920 | St. Leo College |
| 1920–1923 | St. Leo College High School |
| 1923–1927 | St. Leo Academy |
| 1927–1929 | Benedictine High School |
| 1929–1964 | Saint Leo College Preparatory School |
| 1959–1999 | Saint Leo College |
| 1999 | Saint Leo University |

**Pssst . . .**

Psst. . . . "Saint" both abbreviated and spelled out is not a typo. According to Sister Dorothy, O.S.B., the current librarian and archivist, the College used to abbreviate the word "Saint" up until the late 1920s.

College Cheer

RICKETY, RACKETY,
CLICKETY, CLACKETY,
SIS-BOOM-BAH!
SAINT LEO COLLEGE,
RAH! RAH! RAH!

*The **first** official college cheer, circa 1908–1909*
From Saint Leo Abbey Archives

*In sum, the process of values education involves clarifying, modeling, teaching, asking you to role model values, and to apply them in your educational, personal, and professional life. The next chapter will show you the long road that educators have taken over the years to bring you to the place where your online education is fused with your values.*

*Whew!*
From Siobhan Herkert

# CHAPTER 2

# THE ROAD TO VALUES EDUCATION

The road to educating students effectively has been long and winding. From preschool to postsecondary, in public and private schools, curricula across areas of study have been rerouted and remapped to better educate students. In particular, over the past fifteen years values, character virtues, and ethics, once a common part of education for students in years past, have reappeared after some very significant changes in the social and political climate of the time. Let's take a look back at what education would have been like for you if you were a student in 19th-century America.

First of all, the Bible would have been a common source of readings in both public and private schools at all levels. You would have most likely started the day with a prayer. In your early grades, you would have learned to read with the McGuffey readers whose stories focused on character development and virtuous behaviors.

McGuffey's Eclectic Primer *by William H. McGuffey, 1879.*

**Fall 1974**
*Off-campus continuing education Centers opened in Virginia.*

**Fall 1975**
*Off-campus continuing education Centers opened in Georgia, Florida, South Carolina, and Louisiana.*

**February 15, 1980**
*Henderson Hall renamed after Charles F. Henderson, graduate of the college, who died of cancer at age 24.*

**July 1, 1985**
**Dr. Daniel Henry**, *former vice president for administration at the University of Dayton, became the* **sixth** *college president and served for two years.*

From Siobhan Herkert

If you were fortunate enough to attend college, you would have discovered a curriculum with roots going back to the colonial period when students had a rigid list of courses in Latin, Greek, logic, and rhetoric. Scientific courses of study and mathematics entered later, but electives and independent study were unknown. You would have found that prayers and church services were common. In fact, even late into the 19th century in many colleges "compulsory religious exercises equaled literary exercises" (Rudolph, 75). As the century came to a close, colleges like Johns Hopkins, Harvard, and Stanford as well as state universities abandoned mandatory church services for voluntary ones (77).

As changes in college curriculum occurred, so did changes in primary and secondary schools. Many of the changes in public education in the United States were led by Horace Mann (1756–1859), a social reformer who argued that children should learn together in "common" public schools which would provide equal learning opportunities for all. Most historians, in fact, credit Mann with the birth of public education.

**February 22, 1986**
Sister Germaine Bevans, O.S.B. elected prioress of Holy Name Monastery.

**November 14, 1986**
Expansion of Cannon Memorial Library.

**February 13, 1987**
**Monsignor Frank M. Mouch,** former director of education for the Diocese of Saint Petersburg and rector of a seminary in Ohio, appointed by the board of trustees as **seventh** president.

**January 1994**
Saint Leo began to offer graduate degree programs in Business Administration.

Horace Mann and the leaders of the common school movement argued forcefully for the importance of moral training for all young people in order to make democracy work. Even though the U.S. Constitution required a separation of church and state, public education continued to embrace character development as a main goal of schooling. And even until the 1950s, college and university presidents were typically religious leaders, even at state universities. They argued that a critical nature of their role was to develop young men (and eventually women) of character.

Schools across America opened every day with a prayer until a U.S. Supreme Court decision in 1962 banned public prayer and Bible reading in public schools.

Up until that time character education was tied to values that often overlapped with religious values. No one questioned the appropriateness of this practice until the Supreme Court ruling. Although many schools fought the ruling (and to this day many rural public schools, where no one objects, begin with a prayer), it was constitutional law. Teachers became cautious about anything that sounded religious in their teachings. School districts were very careful to avoid any implication of favoring any religious activity in their policies. As a result, and in conjunction with other events that emphasized individualism of the 1960s and 1970s (Vietnam War protests, Free Speech Movement, Civil Rights Movement), character education began to decline. Textbooks steered away from any focus that sounded like preaching, and teachers were taught to steer clear of teaching values.

Horace Mann

In this climate, a new idea, **values clarification** (Simon & Kirschenbaum, 1972), grew in popularity in secondary schools and colleges. In this method of instruction, teachers were trained to help you decide on your own what you believed, not to impose prescribed attitudes on you. Although the movement reached its height during the 60s and 70s, it was actually influenced by an earlier figure in education, **John Dewey** (1859–1952), the University of Chicago philosopher and moral educator. Dewey was considered the father of American progressive education in the early part of the 20th century. His beliefs about moral education influenced those who supported values clarification. Dewey's advocates assert that it is the *process* of education that is more important than the *product* of education. Learning how to resolve a conflict is of higher value than the actual decision itself. What is right is usually defined by what is most practical and what is best for the majority. This belief is at the root of values clarification.

The past 15 years have seen a resurgence of the integration of values, character virtues, and ethics in the school curriculum in all disciplines and at all levels of schooling, from preschool through college. The renewed popularity of values education began with the "rebirth" of character education (Lickona, 1993) in the late 1980s as a response to dissatisfaction with the "me" spiritedness of the 1970s and early 1980s.

*February 1998*
Center for Online Learning
(COL) established.

*Fall 1995*
Continuing education centers
opened in North Florida.

*September 8, 1995*
Faculty office building
renamed DeChantal Hall in
honor of Sr. DeChantal.

*Fall 1996*
A second master's degree
program began in education to
offer an M.Ed in Education
Leadership or Instructional
Leadership.

From Siobhan Herkert

Actually, character education had never *died*. It had been temporarily replaced by an alternative (in part in response to Supreme Court decisions to restrict the role of religion in schools). This alternative was called **moral reasoning education**. The approach, which emphasizes individualism, succeeded in part because of the American national mood. Its success can also be attributed to the growth of cognitive psychology, which studies in part how we acquire our thoughts and ideas and how we use that knowledge. With the growth of this field of study, psychologists and educators applied theories of cognitive psychology to how we think and develop as moral individuals. *But with two roads in front of them, which road would educators finally take?* The decision between character education and moral reasoning was yet to come.

To understand the debate more clearly, let's look in more depth at character education and moral reasoning. Here's a definition of character education:

> **Character education** is the deliberate, proactive effort to develop good character in kids—or, more simply, to teach children right from wrong. It assumes that right and wrong do exist, that there are objective moral standards that transcend individual choice—standards like respect, responsibility, honesty, and fairness—and that we should teach these directly to young people (Lickona, 11).

Character education is more closely aligned with the elementary school, with many specific curricular programs that offer a "character trait a week."

However, especially in the past ten years, character education has found proponents at secondary and post secondary institutions.

From Siobhan Herkert

> **Moral reasoning education** advocates agree that developing good character in children and young adults is a highly valuable goal for education. However, they argue that for you to develop good character, you must first develop the skill to reason. To help you develop reasoning skills that can be applied to moral decision-making, moral reasoning educators use stories and real world events that are designed specifically to trigger critical thinking and personal reflection. They believe that education is a process where you learn as you interact in meaningful ways with the world and with ideas, making sense of things in your own personal way. The teacher is a guide who uses discovery and inquiry techniques to aid you in seeing the various sides of

**Fall 1997**
Dr. Arthur F. Kirk, Jr.,
former president of Keuka
College in New York, became
the **eighth** college president of
Saint Leo.

**April 1998**
Baseball stadium named in
honor of late Dr. Southard,
former president of Saint Leo.

**May 3, 1998**
Saint Leo College conferred
Honorary Doctorate of
Humane Letters upon Sr.
DeChantal.

**July 1998**
Sister Mary Clare Neuhofer,
O.S.B. became prioress (and
currently in this position at the
Holy Name Monastery).

moral issues and forming personal conclusions based on solid reasoning. The teacher's job is to stimulate effective thinking about moral issues; using known procedures for logical, rational argument and perhaps to get you to consider alternatives to beliefs you inherited from your parents and immediate community. Even college teachers at denominational institutions usually believe their role is to "shake things up and pull students out of their comfort zone" (Colby, 2000). Moral reasoning advocates tend to be teachers of older students, high school and college, not surprisingly due in part to younger children's more limited abilities to analyze at these higher levels.

Let's take an example of a moral reasoning strategy to see it in action. Imagine that last term a friend took the same course as you are currently taking. The week an assignment is due, your kids got sick and your boss assigned you extra work. You tell your friend that you won't be able to complete your assignment for class. Since the assignment has not changed, he offers you the assignment he turned in last term and for which he received an A. According to this school of thought, your decision will reflect one of a number of stages in your moral development. These stages, developed by Harvard psychologist **Lawrence Kohlberg,** move from simple to more complex moral reasoning and look like this:

Stage 1: Avoidance of Punishment; "Will I Get in Trouble?"

Stage 2: Tit-for-Tat Fairness; "What's in It for Me?"

Stage 3: Interpersonal Loyalty; "What Will People Think of Me?"

Stage 4: Concern for Social Consequences; "What if Everybody Did It?"

Stage 5: Respect the Rights of Every Person; "What Makes for a Good Society?"

Stage 6: Universal Principles; "What Are the Principles by Which We Achieve Justice?"

From Siobhan Herkert

Sources: http://www.ccp.uchicago.edu/grad/Joseph_Craig/kohlberg.htm
http://faculty.plts.edu/gpence/html/kohlberg.htm.

Let's say your decision to our scenario is to submit your own incomplete assignment rather than turn in your friend's as your own. A moral reasoning approach to the dilemma would ask you to examine the reason *behind* your decision. Were you afraid to get caught? (Stage 1) Were you concerned about your personal reputation if someone found out what you had done? (Stage 3) Or perhaps you concluded that taking your friend's assignment would violate the professor's trust in you and your own integrity (Stage 4). Your instructor would facilitate your understanding of your moral development by helping you progress through the "answers" you chose to the dilemma based on your reasons. Purposely, no dilemma would have a clear-cut right or wrong answer.

Beyond his work in developing a methodology for moral reasoning used by schools, Lawrence Kohlberg also advocated what he called "the just community," where the emphasis was on group deliberation through regular class meetings (1985). The goal of a just community is shared consensus, where decisions are based on reasoning skills, not dictated universal truths. While this created an open, more liberal forum, which called

**October 1998**
Center for Catholic/Jewish studies established. COL offers first online class.

**May 10, 1999**
Rev. Marion Richard Bowman, O.S.B. died at the age of 93.

**August 24, 1999**
Saint Leo College became Saint Leo University.

**September 1, 2000**
First COL graduate.

upon students to think carefully through their decisions in the classroom, the mood of the country began to change in the mid-1980s and the pendulum began to swing back toward the conservative. A number of events affected this reversal, including the Reagan White House, Japanese superiority in technology (and by implication in education), a conservative Supreme Court, and the publication of *A Nation at Risk* in 1983. The latter document sent high school and school district administrators scurrying to refocus the curriculum on the five "new" basics (language, math, science, social studies, and technology). Nonetheless, educators were still fearful of direct instruction of values; moral education was not one of the five basics. In 1986 *Newsweek* magazine described "morals education" as a "minefield" because there was no consensus on "which values" should be taught. A summary of research on moral education in 1987 concluded that values clarification methods had had no significant impact on the moral development of students. However, the principles of cognitive psychology did reinforce the conclusion that "moral knowledge is commensurate with interactive rather than directive educational practices" (Nucci, 1987). Such conflicting early research made the educational road still more complicated.

In 1989 President George Bush convened the first education summit of the state governors. This meeting started the standards movement that has dominated K–12 education for the past fifteen years. This same year, Harvard psychiatrist **Robert Coles** published the results of a survey of the moral life of children and young adults. Among the results of this study, Coles found that:

- 65% of high school students would cheat if they thought they could get away with it,
- nearly 20% of junior and senior high school students in poor areas agreed that "suicide is alright, because a person has a right to do what he wants with himself," and
- children from the highest income brackets expressed the greatest uncertainty when confronted with morally ambiguous situations (Coles & Genevie, 1990).

Coles' data led him to conclude that a young person's relationship to God and religion in general is strongly correlated with the moral logic he uses and that his moral assumptions are the basis of how he acts. Yet, only

- 16% of those surveyed attributed a religious base to their moral decisions,
- 18% did something if it felt good,
- 20% looked to parents or another adult,
- 25% did what would be best for the most people, and
- 10% did what would help them personally to get ahead (Coles & Genevie, 1990).

Many people believed that apparently the lack of guidance and direction that characterized the values clarification era had directly influenced the moral development of young people. Coles himself presented the dilemma clearly:

> Teachers struggle everyday with the issues of character but their hands are tied. They can't say what is absolutely wrong, what is evil, without being accused of promoting religion. Once teachers were invested with a kind of moral authority.

**January 8, 2001**
*Cannon Memorial Library unveiled its new information management system.*

**April 26, 2001**
*First Academic Excellence Day celebrated on University Campus.*

**August 2001**
*University students received Apple-i Books for wireless Internet access on campus.*

**September 2002**
*Saint Leo expanded its online degree offerings.*

**January 2003**
*i-ROAR launched.*

> Religion was taught in the schools, and children prayed at the beginning and end of the day. . . . We're not advocating a return to those days, for clearly the line between church and state had become dangerously blurred. But the point remains that when religion was stripped from the schools, nothing came along to take its place, and teachers were stripped of the moral authority they once had (Coles, 46).

A few lone voices tried to put the growing concern about the state of moral education into perspective without trying to promote one method over another. Edwin Delattre, an education professor at Boston University, wrote in an *Education Week* Commentary in 1990 that most value or moral programs "foisted upon schools, teachers, and students" were horrible. Some he lamented were rigid and highly questionable in their authority to define righteous behaviors by "simple" litmus tests (his reference is to the early character education programs). Others, "such as 'values clarification' are based on mindless reduction of morality to a matter of personal and arbitrary taste . . . that teach students nothing about the real nature of principled judgment and conduct" (Delattre, 1990). He argued that real moral education occurs in the way teachers and adults behave and "real moral deliberation presupposes learning habits of integrity: what can be taught is the principle of intellectual rigor and reliable thought as applied to questions of all kinds" (Delattre, 1990).

But Coles' data were too impressive to be ignored by the layman and left to intellectual debate among professors. The country was ready for debate. What came to take the place of religion in public educational institutions was **character education** for K–12 schools and **communitarianism** for colleges.

**Amitai Etzioni**, a George Washington University sociologist, is a leader in the rebirth of the return to directive values instruction that began in the early 1990s and the growth of the philosophy of communitarianism. The goal of the communitarian movement is restoration of civility and commitment to "the common good." A primary goal of education and ethics is to develop citizens who will put the best interests of everyone over their personal best interests. Etzioni challenges what he calls "excesses" of liberty (personal interests) and specifically criticizes the American Civil Liberties Union, which blocked drug testing, sobriety checks, and disclosure of those carrying the AIDS virus (1992). In 1991, **Arthur Schlesinger, Jr.,** a Pulitzer Prize-winning Harvard historian and advisor to President Kennedy, suggested in *The Disuniting of America: Reflections on a Multicultural Society,* that the increasing emphasis on valuing subcultures' identities in the United States could lead to a disintegration of common values that makes Americans a community. Schlesinger concluded the Foreword to his book with, "In a world savagely rent by ethnic and racial antagonisms, it is all the more essential that the United States continue as an example of how a highly differentiated society holds itself together (p. 20)." Americans, he believes, must put America first. **John Gardner**, president of the University of California at Berkeley, describes a vision of America that embraces diversity, not through dictating common values, but through the emphasizing of the value of community (1991). All three of these communitarians urge educators at all levels to put teaching the core values that made America great back into the curriculum. Etzioni argues for a directive instructional approach. Schlesinger urges history teachers to thoughtfully balance the contributions of groups with mainline tradition to make America a well-mixed salad bowl. And Gardner challenges Americans to see the greater community as the model for moral growth.

**August 2003**
State of the art residence halls
opened on university campus.

**September 2004**
Twenty-year anniversary for
"Time Warp" the faculty band
on university campus.

**October 2004**
COL graduates their
1000th student.

**November 2004**
University extends campus
offices into the larger
community of Dade City.

Helen Haste later described the communitarian movement's growth in contrast to the philosophy of the 1970s:

> Communitarian thinkers start from a very different . . . psychological tradition. They emphasize the primacy of language and social interaction in the generation of meaning . . . for communitarians the community's social functions are also a source of morality. Social order rests on people's interdependence, and society only functions if people recognize and act upon their community responsibilities. It works both ways; in order for the state to function, individuals must cooperate; in order for the individual to thrive (indeed to survive), the state must be effective (1998, p. 3).

Hillary Rodham Clinton, first lady in the 1990s and a U.S. senator, has been a strong believer in communitarianism. Her proverb that, "it takes a whole village to raise a child," calls for "a consensus of values and a common vision of what we can do today, individually and collectively, to build strong families and communities" (1996, p. iii). Another outspoken political figure in the communitarian movement has been William Bennett, former Secretary of Education under Ronald Reagan. His work, *The Book of Virtues* (Bennett, 1993), contains tales, from biblical stories to political legends and speeches, which reinforce values that he believes made the American dream come true—self-discipline, compassion, work, responsibility, friendship, courage, perseverance, honesty, loyalty, and faith.

The moral reasoning/individualists, however, may perceive this communitarianism attitude to be detrimental to self-knowledge. Asserting that to develop skills in reasoning, you must also develop self-knowledge. Philosopher Ann Russell Mayeaux (1993) even went so far as to argue that the excesses of community led to fascism. She stated that such extremes could only be safeguarded when you take personal responsibility for your fellowman or woman—and personal responsibility for others begins with personal knowledge.

While philosophers like Mayeaux assert the importance of personal knowledge, however, communitarians would propose that too much "self" can be a dangerous thing, creating among other things selfishness, egotism, and an inability to view yourself as part of a greater whole. It may further cause too much confidence in reason as the only tool to solve problems. (Haste, 1998, 5).

*But the arguments are not finished.* Still other thinkers assert that the character education movement (and by implication of the communitarianism philosophy) is dependent upon a rather bleak view of children:

> Character education's "fix-the-kids" orientation follows logically from the belief that kids need fixing. Indeed, the movement seems to be driven by a stunningly dark view of children—and, for that matter, of people in general. . . . In fact, at least three assumptions seem to be at work when the need for self-control is stressed: First, that we are all at war not only with others but with ourselves, torn between our desires and our reason (or social norms); second, that these desires are fundamentally selfish, aggressive, or otherwise unpleasant; and third, that these desires are very strong, constantly threatening to overpower us if we don't rein them in. Collectively, these statements describe religious dogma, not scientific fact. Indeed, the evidence from several disciplines converge to cast doubt on this sour view of human beings and, instead, supports the idea that it is as "natural" for children to help as to hurt (Kohn, 1997, 431).

Kohn's and other's concerns about character education and a philosophy rooted in what he describes as a pessimistic view of humanity were small voices, however, in the dominance of the communitarian movement and character education culture of the 1990s. It was a decade of economic abundance for most Americans, yet it ended with increasing concerns about economic stability and fears of international terrorism. Not unlike the 1950s, the country held fast to its values and defended itself with relatively conservative philosophies regarding moral education. High school and college students' values also reflected the era's nature. *Service projects* participation increased dramatically in late high school and early college, from a low of 66% of college freshmen in 1989 to a record high of 83% in 2001 (Cooperative Institutional Research Program [CIRP] data on 400,000 freshmen from 700 colleges, Sax, 2003). During that same period, however, college freshmen's commitments to social activism and political issues declined. These results may reflect a greater quantity of opportunities for service projects (through grants and more numbers of programs, which also reflect the increased societal emphasis on promoting values). The increased college emphasis in admissions applications on community service (a reflection of educators' priorities) should also be noted. Statements by college students over the past five years express disconnectedness from state, federal, or international politics, but are positive about service experiences that lead to a feeling they can make a difference at a local level (Sax, 2003). Interestingly, in the early 1990s, community service was exactly the antidote promoted by many educators and politicians as the way to spearhead values education in the schools (Townsend, 1992). Developing good character through personally meaningful experiences has apparently become valued by you, your peers, and your teachers, but engaging in political conflicts to try to change "amoral" governmental policies like your counterparts of the late 1960s has not.

So we have taken a long road to see that perhaps this is the right time to bring the communitarians and character educators together to join hands with the individualists and moral reasoning educators. Both character education and moral reasoning attempt to develop character in individuals, one through identifying basic and universally accepted moral standards, the other by progressing students through more complex stages of moral reasoning. The debate between the two views has softened since the turn of the 21st century. Perhaps events of 9/11 and the fears of terrorism based on bigotry and misunderstanding have given weight to *both* sides of the values education debate, whose advocates may now realize they both desire the same goals. Perhaps the emergence of service learning where you learn to apply what you have learned in class to real-life situations has also helped. **The program at Saint Leo University is a good example of the blending of character and moral reasoning education.** Two of the six Saint Leo core values represent the two opposing approaches: *Personal Development* (individualism/moral reasoning) and *Community* (communitarianism/character education). A third core value, *Responsible Stewardship,* describes how the other two come together and represents the general trend across the country in increased emphasis on community service and service learning.

The remainder *of this book* will focus in detail on values integrated in the general education course of study. Each chapter will begin with a set of quotations that reflect the varied interpretations of the core value. A set of reflection questions will follow to prompt you to ask how the value affects you personally. Finally, activities for each value by discipline will be provided as suggestions for you to consider.

# Afterword

## Values: The Key to Your Success

Questioning the place of values in the undergraduate curriculum today seems to some almost pointless, almost silly. In a world beset with ethical questions and problems, clearly every college educated person needs to be exposed to a set of core values, challenged to understand those values, and in turn educated about the central mission that values will play in shaping a successful individual. Educated people today must know what rests at their core and must be able to grapple with the values that guide and motivate them. Unless our students leave our campuses with that fundamental ability, they will be unable to find an employer whose values fit their own and with whom they can successfully work.

Yet, with that said, traditionalists on many campuses persist in asking why we do not simply leave the issue of values to student life professionals on our campuses. For these people, beset with the problem of how to teach ever increasing amounts of data in every field, the question of how to fit anything more into the curriculum is paramount. Traditionalists assert that in a world where the half life of knowledge in every discipline is shrinking every day, keeping curriculum current can be achieved only through adding credits or adding a fifth year to the undergraduate curriculum. For them, adding values means adding another burden to their already packed syllabi—at the expense of something else.

Traditionalists also question the need to add values to a curriculum that seems to already be overloaded with extraneous materials. Those studying the Millennials—the new students who are coming to our campuses—point out this generation and particularly their parents, are intent upon gaining a practical education, an education that will allow them to step quickly into successful career tracks. An additional computer course, an internship, or even an integrated work experience would seem more important to them. Even those who understand the need to have a values basis for living a life well, do not necessarily quickly embrace the idea that a values-based education is also the foundation for gaining "the good life." Again, the addition of values seems unnecessary, even burdensome. Values, after all, will not better train the budding computer scientist or the new accountant bent on demonstrating a mastery of ever-evolving and new computer languages, or new approaches to profit and loss statements mandated by yet another federal regulation. Adding a course in values would be bad enough; adding a careful examination of how values shape our approaches to knowledge is even worse. The addition of values across the curriculum will, for traditionalists, mean the loss of time from essential new additions to their fields.

For yet others, the question of how values shape our knowledge, our selection of what we choose to learn and what we choose to teach is also uncomfortable. After all, values-based education is not something we learned in graduate school. And, as Leon Botstein reminds us, ". . . there is a generalized fear, not of religion per se, but of doctrine linked to any particular religious purpose" often presented in the guise of a values-laden education (Botstein, *Jefferson's Children: Education and the Promise of American Culture,* 80). Besides, can values even be taught? Can we successfully design a curriculum that has as an integral part, student learning and the development of a values structure? Can we balance values-laden questions with the free inquiry that must be a part of any college education? Researchers and others have grappled with these questions. Their conclusions seem consistent: *yes,* we can accomplish our task but only if we succeed in creating a curriculum where values are a part of all courses and a part of the lived nature of the college community that students experience. *Values, then, must become a regular part of the whole organizational culture to be a successful part of the curriculum that will shape students.*

So, why not just leave values alone? Why burden everyone with one more uncomfortable item in the already crowded curriculum, the already packed syllabus? The answer, of course, is easy. If we want our students to succeed in life, to do well, then we have an obligation to bring values into our curriculum, not as a course that stands alone in a "once and done" approach to values, but as an integral part of all of the courses we teach. In this approach, an approach we might label 'values across the curriculum,' we will help students understand that the struggle to address questions of values permeates everything they do. Once students understand that, then they will have gained an education rather than a simple training. By being educated, they will be capable of bringing a systematic approach to the creation of values to their lives, enabling them to embrace the values-laden culture that they will enter after graduation.

So why, finally, add values to an undergraduate curriculum? Focusing on values is critical if we want students who are educated and ready to face the world with the confidence rather than graduates who will have no framework into which they can insert new knowledge that they can use successfully in a changing world.

Perhaps an easy way to understand the value of values is to revisit the long raging debate over why American higher education, by passionately clinging to a liberal arts core for everything we do, remains the best higher education system in the world. By briefly reexamining the question of why the liberal arts is critical as the foundation to every major, we will clarify the reasons we must also add values and values study to the undergraduate educational experience. Unlike the narrow focus brought to the end of an undergraduate education through mastery in an individual discipline, the liberal arts—art, art history, philosophy, religion, literature, languages, history, anthropology, psychology, political science, sociology, the natural sciences, and math—teach students to make the connection between the life of the mind and the world of work. The liberal arts prepare our students to join the ever shrinking world of commerce, both online and on the ground as individuals with the dexterity of mind needed to make choices about careers and to change careers as the world they enter evolves at an almost revolutionary speed.

Liberal arts disciplines teach our students how to think, the essential skill for a technological world where many of the jobs of which will occupy today's students have yet to be even dreamed. In a utilitarian era where the focus has fallen to first jobs rather than careers and education is easily replaced by career training, explaining why the liberal arts are essential to success is essential for all of us in higher education. None of us should forget lessons learned by earlier graduates and lessons taught back to us by them. The liberal arts are both central and essential to any successful business career that emerges in a highly technical world. Nick Corcodilos, author and founder of North Bridge Group, Inc., a leading international job placement firm, reminds us that the liberal arts educated student

**SAINT LEO ALMA, 1967**

From Saint Leo Abbey Archives

**SAINT LEO ALMA MATER, PRESENT DAY**

From Saint Leo Abbey Archives

possesses many of the fundamental skills and attributes that the nonliberal arts educated competition may lack. For example, the liberal arts and by extension values laden curricular models allow students to develop:

## SKILLS

- Defining problems and tasks,
- Mastery of information retrieval systems (e.g., library books, periodicals, internet, personal interviews),
- Planning and executing research,
- Organizing ideas and solutions,
- Writing and communicating, and
- Perhaps most important, a well-honed ability to learn what you need to accomplish a task.

*Source: Corcodilos, Nick, A. (1997). Ask the headhunter: Reinventing the interview to win the job. New York: Penguin Books.*

Corcodilos also posits that the values enriched liberal arts educated student will be able to demonstrate the following attributes:

- an open mind to new ideas and approaches
- disciplined work habits
- a critical eye and ear

In other words, liberal arts students will have the skills and attributes they need to become successful, and these same attributes flow from a values enriched curriculum. Indeed, as the values activities in this book demonstrate, the values laden approach to teaching and learning extends the benefits derived from the liberal arts to technical and professional fields by demanding that students and their teachers examine fundamental principles in every discipline. By explicitly recognizing the need to conduct that sophisticated examination of values, the student and the teacher must together confront the choice of one value or set of values over another. Rather than being passive in learning, the process of informed choice demands an active approach to learning.

Research has consistently shown over time that the liberal arts graduate, the person grounded in a values-based education, in the end succeeds at a higher rate than those who are simplistically technically trained. Indeed, the National Association of College Employers (NACE) discovered that the ten personal qualities that employers seek are:

1. Communication skills
2. Motivation/initiative
3. Teamwork skills
4. Leadership skills
5. Academic achievement/GPA
6. Interpersonal skills
7. Flexibility/adaptability
8. Technical skills
9. Honesty/integrity
10. A tie between work ethic and analytical and problem-solving skills

*Source: National Association of Colleges and Employers (2000).* Job outlook 2000—what employers want *(Retrieved from: http://www.naceweb.org).*

So where does that lead us? The previous chapter notes that, "the past 15 years have seen a resurgence of integration of values, character virtues, and ethics in the school curriculum in all disciplines and at all levels of schooling, from preschool through post secondary. . . ." Unfortunately, so much of that helpful resurgence has come with political baggage that

many reject. Indeed, values can, in the hands of purveyors of left or right ideologies grounded in one or the others' ideas of political correctness, degenerate into dogma that destroys learning if values are seen only as a set of beliefs upheld by a certain segment of the population. But values transcend the ideologies of either right or left and form the basis for success in life. As such, then, values are available to students of all political persuasions, available as guiding principles that allow the educated person to move beyond dogma to a self-examined life.

To be effective, then, the core values we pass on to our students need to be examined. These should be values that students integrate into their lives in ways that will enable them to make informed choices in their work. These core values—values that can capture an individual's and an organization's soul—should be easily recalled and lead to appropriate actions. The values based revival in the Saint Leo University curriculum was inspired by coherent organizational planning and assessment processes. The introduction of values as central to the learning and operational cultures of the University lead to a stronger academic environment, one that students find more appealing. By making the core values integral to all levels of university decision making, from budget planning to personnel review, as well as inculcating core values into the curriculum, the culture of the community has been transformed in many positive ways. As educators Peter Drucker and James Collins both point out, the same kind of examined values lead to the same results for individuals and for the corporations for whom they work.

*So why study values?* Why jump back into moral education, a dilemma fraught with dangers particularly when it gets wrapped up in any kind of religious identification? American values, the basis the American Republic was founded on, are critical to our continued success as a society and to the individual student's success as a worker within that society. Examined values that can stand the test of clear articulation and intense scrutiny in a classroom are critical to understanding personal, corporate, and societal needs. For values can stand up to careful scrutiny and serve us as measures against which we can make sound decisions.

In short, values arrived at, through thoughtful deliberative processes, become the key to greater success in life. A long legacy of thinkers in our history testifies to this important point: Thomas Jefferson stated that we need to teach values to all of our students, all of our citizens so that they, as a literate and educated citizenry, can make intelligent rational decisions for our country's continued success. Teddy Roosevelt lectured from his "bully pulpit" on the need to believe in core values, in American values that allow us to question authority in a structured way so that we can in fact make progress. And in our own time corporate leaders like former General Electric CEO Jack Welch or current Home Depot CEO Robert Nardelli tell us that without a firm sense of values we cannot hope to succeed in the world of business.

Only by asking questions from a values-driven moral stance is progress possible. The case, then, is clear: American education and future corporate success rest on the basic premise that *values are the key*.

*Where does this lead me?*
From Saint Leo Abbey Archives

# PHOTO GALLERY

## SLU SPORTS TEAMS OF THE PAST

*Basketball team*

From Saint Leo Abbey Archives

*Golf team*

From Saint Leo Abbey Archives

*Academic and Social Cultures for Online Learners*

*Soccer team*

*Swimming team*

Football team

From Saint Leo Abbey Archives

Football squad

From Saint Leo Abbey Archives

*Brothers and candidates in 1893*

From Saint Leo Abbey Archives

*The sisters of Saint Leo Abbey in the 1890s*

From Saint Leo Abbey Archives

*Post card from Saint Leo catalog, 1897–1898*

From Saint Leo Abbey Archives

*The 1900 St. Leo military march*

From Saint Leo Abbey Archives

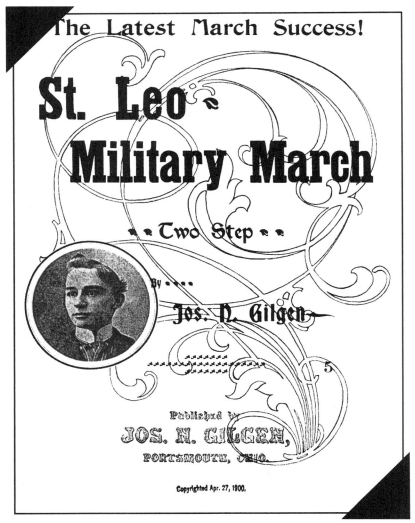

From Saint Leo Abbey Archives

*Boating on Lake Jovita in the 1900s*

From Saint Leo Abbey Archives

*Railroad depot in 1908*

From Saint Leo Abbey Archives

*First study hall*

From Saint Leo Abbey Archives

*Inauguration of Gym, 1945*

From Saint Leo Abbey Archives

*Theatre production of earlier years*

From Saint Leo Abbey Archives

*Abbey cafeteria*

From Saint Leo Abbey Archives

*Saint Leo Campus*

From Saint Leo Abbey Archives

First class of 1959

From Saint Leo Abbey Archives

Classroom circa, early 1960s

From Saint Leo Abbey Archives

*Cheerleaders in the 1960s*

From Saint Leo Abbey Archives

*Leo the Lion, 1960s*

From Saint Leo Abbey Archives

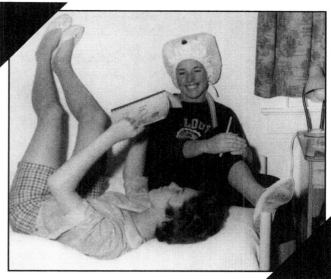

*Girls dorm, 1960s*

From Saint Leo Abbey Archives

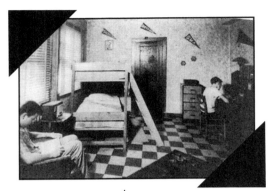

*Prep dorm, 1960s*
From Fr. Malachy Maguire Collection

*Pink Elephant Canteen*
*St. Edward Hall, 1960s*
From Fr. Malachy Maguire Collection

*The Holy Name Priory and monks of Saint Leo Abbey in the 1980s*
From Fr. Malachy Maguire Collection

## SAINT LEO UNIVERSITY, PRESENT DAY

*Lion at main entrance*
From Lorrie Zelakowski

*The Walk of Saint Leo time capsule*
From Saint Leo Abbey Archives

*Lake Jovita*
From Saint Leo Abbey Archives

*Saint Leo Abbey*

From Lorrie Zelakowski

*Abbey Church*

From Lorrie Zelakowski

*Stained glass in Abbey Church*

From Lorrie Zelakowski

# CHAPTER 3

# SUPPORTING ONLINE

# LEARNERS

*Pssst . . .*

Remember to
checkout the textboxes
for a look back at
Saint Leo!

Obtaining a degree is an important commitment, and, like the students in the scenarios you will be reading, finding an institution that meets your educational needs can be a huge undertaking. Saint Leo University provides its students with the opportunity to earn a degree and to obtain a values-based education. As you read in the preface, this book will help you understand how essential values are to your academic, professional, and personal life. This chapter was written specifically to demonstrate how a values based education can be integrated into online learning. Attending Saint Leo in a virtual environment poses unique challenges. Students must be self-motivated and dedicated to achieving their goal. With its core values, the university provides an atmosphere that educates in mind, body, and spirit, fostering values as a part of one's education and life. You'll read more about the concepts of values-based education as they relate to the academic, professional and personal aspects of a Saint Leo student.

*Theresa is 31, a mother of three working part-time and raising her family with her husband Roberto. Their children are 12, 10, and 7 years of age. Theresa started college right after high school but delayed finishing so she and Roberto could get married and start a family. Theresa has always wanted to finish her degree and now that her children are all in school and a little older, she feels this is the time to make her dream come true. Her first commitment is to her family and then her studies. She was a very good student during her first two years in college and with 72 transfer credits, she is excited to get restarted and finish her degree before her oldest son is a junior in high school. Theresa wants to set a good example for all her children but especially hopes her decision to finish her degree will help motivate her son to go on to college.*

## REFLECTION QUESTIONS

1. Theresa has a term paper due and because of family and work challenges, did not have much time to work on it. She searches the internet for the topic that she chose and finds a document that could satisfy her term paper. What are some of the moral challenges that she will face as she attempts to complete her assignment on time? Post your responses to the class discussion board.

2. Theresa was excited about participating in the weekly discussions that her professor posted to the class message board. The day after she posted her opinion another student in her class responded and strongly disagreed with her position on the topic. How might she respond to that student?

3. What roles does **integrity** and **respect** play in the above situations?

# ACADEMIC

It has been said that the true test of who we are is what we do when we are alone. At times like these when our morals and values are paramount in influencing our decisions. In an online learning environment there are numerous opportunities where it is solely up to you as to whether or not you will succeed academically. While you may have the support and guidance of a professor and fellow students, the influence of peers and the observant eye of others are not present as they would be in a 'grounded' classroom setting. For students like Theresa, the commitments and pressures of a marriage, children, and a job are real, but the need to serve as an example to those who look up to you can motivate you to do your absolute best. In this way, the core values of Saint Leo University can assist your pur-

Is it history or hearsay?

Saint Leo Preparatory students used to sleep outside in sleeping bags next to the two cement lion statues.

**It's history.** The students used to sleep there in the 1940s and 1950s to protect them from vandalism. Father Marion Bowman had the lions removed in the 1960s. Then in July 2000, two lions were a gift from the class of 1954.

*Present-day statue of one Lion*
From Lorrie Zelakowski

Is it history or hearsay?

Father Marion Bowman, O.S.B., attended Saint Leo College Preparatory and graduated as class valedictorian. He later taught math and science.

**It's history.** In 1954 Father Bowman was named the third abbot of Saint Leo and later served as president of the college. In 1970 the gym was named the Marion Bowman Activities Center to honor him.

*Father Marion Bowman, O.S.B.*
From Saint Leo Abbey Archives

suit to earn a higher education. The need to draw upon the values of **excellence, respect, and integrity** resound in the virtual classroom.

For example, as a student you are faced with completing your assignments, preparing for exams, and participating in asynchronous message board discussions and synchronous chat sessions. The need to do your best and approach these educational requirements with **excellence** and **integrity** are essential. In return, you nourish elements of your personal values, not only during your time as a student but also for the rest of your life. Your sense of **integrity** will also be challenged when completing online assignments and examinations, as the convenience and accessibility of the internet as a source of information can tempt you to be dishonest and not produce original work. The advent of the internet and technology make it convenient for information to be shared and accessible. You as a students must resist these temptations, especially those of plagiarism and cheating. That resistance can come only from a strong sense of personal **integrity** and a genuine desire for **excellence.** The institutional academic honor code can also guide you as you strive to be a person of intellectual **integrity.**

The educational journey inevitably surrounds you with the thoughts and opinions of others. One of the pleasures of higher learning is the opportunity to consider different viewpoints and exchange ideas. Online learning lends itself to various modes of unique synchronous and asynchronous discussions of different topics in various disciplines which will furnish you many opportunities to read and react to the opinions of others. The call for respect in these situations is high and, when absent, can erode the classroom environment. Students and professors are called to a standard of **respect** in an environment where the written word is almost forever etched whether it is in an e-mail, on a discussion board, or in a transcripted chatroom.

Saint Leo University's academic policies and procedures exist to foster a values-infused environment. As a student you have the opportunity for personal growth as you are called to a higher standard. In the virtual learning environment, students like Theresa will be faced daily with decisions that call upon their personal morals. When these morals are coupled with the call of the institutional core values, the potential benefits are immeasurable.

*Sarah is 38 and ready to retire from the Army. She is seeking a degree in computer information systems. She feels she needs to obtain her bachelor's degree even though she has been working with computer systems her entire military career. She feels she needs this degree to make her more marketable as she readies herself to enter the job force. She is very concerned about increasing her professional skills and wonders how she will make such a huge career change after all these years in the military. She has taken a course here and there during her military career but is now stationed at a base without a university nearby. She worries that the courses she took before may not count toward her degree or help her professionally. She is concerned about how her current skills will look as she readies herself for the switch into the business and technology field.*

## PROFESSIONAL

Individuals pursuing an online education may be doing so for many different reasons. Whether you are embarking on your first journey down the career path or you are looking for a fresh start in the same or a totally new career, a higher education can bring that career within reach. Think about Sarah. Many students like her are faced with needing that degree to advance in today's workplace despite their years of experience. Regardless of the

*Saint Leo College baseball team of 1909–1910*
From Saint Leo Abbey Archives

motivation to obtain a degree, your education at Saint Leo can assist you in making transitions and achieving your goals.

In support of the core value of **personal development,** Saint Leo University has a number of services and resources for its students. Career Services can assist you in your understanding of which career options exist for you based on the degree program you choose. You can also complete different career assessment surveys that can help you to understand which careers you might be better suited for based on your character, personality, and work preferences. You can then determine how those potential careers match up with your educational pursuits. Finally, Career Services can aid you by providing resume writing tips and web resources that will give you the added edge needed to acquire a good job.

Often, students like Sarah need help in assessing their coursework. For them and for you, your academic advisor is there to help direct you toward the path of your choosing by advising which courses you must take to complete your degree. Academic advising can assist you with many of your educational questions. If factors such as military retirement are facing you, for example, you can obtain academic advising that can help you be a **responsible steward** as you use your military sponsored education to reach your career goals. In the spirit of **responsible stewardship,** Saint Leo University also provides several resources which can evaluate sources of financial aid and Veterans Administration (VA) benefits.

In addition to your advisors, utilize faculty resources. Faculty are experts in your specific career field who bring lifetime experience and transferable skills to your education yet, many students don't make the most of discussing career advancement or career changes with their instructors. Your faculty are available to you during their office hours, as well as during chats that may be held in conjunction with various clubs and organizations. For those pursuing opportunities for leadership advancement, there are co-curricular opportunities such as serving as an officer in an organization or on an advisory board. Additional information regarding these and other professional development opportunities may be found on the schools' website or in its student involvement portal such as iROAR.

The importance of the values of **personal development** and **responsible stewardship** should not be underestimated. Saint Leo University encourages you to understand how these values can shape your dreams and career aspirations.

*James is 45 years old, married with two children in college. He lives in a very small town and drives 30 miles each way to his job as a guard in a corrections facility. He likes his job but would like to learn more about the criminal justice system. James works odd hours and never thought he could take college courses with his schedule. He figures if he takes a class or two online he will be able to see what this online learning environment talk is all about. Several of his friends have taken classes at the university, and his employer will pay for the courses. He wants to see if online education will work for him. Perhaps he can even meet some other students who also work in the criminal justice field.*

## REFLECTION QUESTIONS

1. During James' first term he met students in his classes and attended several of the Student Service chats which helped him adjust and acclimate to the online learning environment. He discovered several other career options by joining the Criminal Justice Organization and is looking into the possibility of changing his career to law enforcement through the encouragement of one of his professors. He is even thinking about running for a position on the Board of Advisors. When he first started he thought he would just take a few classes, but now the possibilities to get involved seem endless. He even wrote his advisor and said, "The online community really surprised me. It was really nice to see that the online community supports my learning." How does this situation relate to our core value of **community**?

2. Go to *The Center for Online Learning* at " *http://64.106.155.33/login/index.asp*

3. Check out the various involvement opportunities available at this site. Which activities might interest you and enhance your **personal development** and sense of belonging to the Saint Leo **community**? Post three of your choices to the class discussion board.

## Personal Life

Online students usually start their academic courses focusing solely on earning a degree. Rarely does the online student think about the personal changes that can take place in a values-centered environment. For many online learners their experience as a Saint Leo student evolves into more than earning a degree. This becomes an opportunity for them to focus on their own personal life journey. South African statesman Nelson Mandela said, "Education is the great engine of personal development. It is through education that the daughter of a peasant can become a doctor, that a son of a mineworker can become the head of the mine, that a child of farm workers can become the president of a great nation." Saint Leo University uses its core values as a foundation for you to gain insight into who you are and who you want to become. A great deal of **personal development** comes from believing in your abilities and pursuing your education despite the every day hurdles of living, like children, career, financial or other personal commitments. Some simply can not find the time or motivation to drive to a campus and sit in a classroom for several hours. Whatever the reason, we encourage you to take time to develop both inside and outside of the classroom and to believe in your own abilities.

A supportive **community** helps you believe in yourself and assists in staying motivated, engaged and connected. Saint Leo University developed its own computer mediated environment called I-ROAR which helps students stay connected. I-ROAR was developed to assist you with out-of-class needs within a virtual environment. I-ROAR is a student involvement portal that stands for Involvement through Redefined Online Activities and Resources. The

Students kept clear of Lake Jovita for fear of rumors of alligators climbing onto shore.

*It's history.* Although there have been no injuries due to alligators, they do inhabit the lake.

In the 1970s, students at Saint Leo enjoyed the bowling lanes located on the campus in the basement of the gym.

*It's history.* There were eight bowling alleys for student use in their free time. They were closed in the 1980s and ten years later a Fitness Center replaced the lanes.

*Alligator in Lake Jovita*
From Saint Leo Abbey Archives

campus mascot, Leo the lion, was the inspiration for its name. From the moment you log on to I-ROAR, you can use this portal and engage in various community building and **personal development** opportunities. James believed that he was simply expanding his horizons by taking a couple of courses, but in actuality he will be able to meet students in situations similar to his own. James will be able to discover an online community where other students, faculty, and staff assist students in learning more about themselves, discovering new interests, meeting new friends, and establishing lifelong connections.

In this unique online student involvement **community** you have the opportunity to serve on committees, hold office in organizations, join clubs, become a reporter or writer for the e-paper, join a book club, or get together with a group of fellow students discussing the latest football scores. I-ROAR exists to support and encourage you as you develop a deeper understanding of Saint Leo University's core values: **excellence, respect, integrity, personal development, stewardship** and **community** and how they can be infused into your personal life. Whether you are 22 or 55 you can always examine the person you are and enhance the person you want to become.

Like the students you met at the beginning of this chapter, you too may have experiences that reflect theirs which have brought you to the College of Online Learning. Yet whatever brings you to this learning environment, we hope you now have a better idea of how a values infused educational experience may contribute to lifelong learning, helping you to develop the knowledge and skills you need for your careers while providing you with the power to develop and live the values that will distinguish you in life.

# The Library, the "Cybrary" and You

The library, known historically as the heart of many an outstanding educational institution, is still at the center of the academic universe today—only, not necessarily are all of its resources or its patrons physically inside. The resources in the **excellent** academic library of today may be on the shelf ready for "check out" and/or they may be in the form of *bits and bytes* on a computer server somewhere very far away. College students and professors, all in pursuit of their own personal academic best, likewise may sit at a study carrel, or be in another classroom or office building on campus, or may be on the other side of the globe. Today's library assignments may involve a scavenger hunt among the microfilm reels and print indexes of the *New York Times* from the 1850s or they may consist of online tours through the "cybrary" of electronic subscription databases. What remains constant is that the best of what is needed to support a college's or university's academic curriculum is still identified, selected, organized, and placed in accessible locations, real and virtual, by highly educated librarians. So, with all of this information either in print or in electronic formats, available in some cases 24 hours a day/7days a week, and with librarians working with students and subject faculty to deliver the best resources, what, you may ask, could possibly be the downside?

> "Excellence costs a great deal."
> *Mary Sarton, The Small Room, 1961*

## REFLECTION QUESTIONS

Reflect on your personal research habits by responding to the following list of questions.

- Where do you turn for your research needs?

- To whom do you go for answers to research questions?

- Name disciplines in which knowledge is organized.

- Are you able to tell the difference between popular and scholarly resources?

- Name some qualities of popular books or magazines or magazine articles.

- Name some qualities of scholarly books or journals or journal articles.

- Name an association of scholars with whom you are familiar.

- Name a researcher or scholar that has impressed you because of his or her commitment to **excellence.**

- With a sea of information out there, how do you find, access, and determine what is suitable and excellent information for your research purpose?

- Do you read the *Help* pages posted in the library for different reference materials or on the web pages of search engines and electronic databases?

- How do you contact a reference librarian?

According to the Pew Internet & American Life Project (*http://www.pewinternet.org/pdfs/PIP_College_Report.pdf*) most college students turn to the internet rather than the library for their research needs.

The internet is a great resource, but unfortunately it lacks any quality control. Anyone can put a webpage on the web. It is a good idea to discuss using internet sources with your professor and your librarian prior to your online information research; there are websites that have merit and there are those that do not. Many professors and librarians nowadays will evaluate and select certain Internet Resources (*http://www.saintleo.edu/SaintLeo/Templates/Inner.aspx?pid=3659*) that have quality content and proven authorship and encourage you to try these websites over randomly selected ones.

Librarians put themselves in your path in order to remind you that they are at your friendly service. They sit at the reference desk or roam the library building or have appointments in online study halls in order to catch you with your question. So, please don't think the librarian is nosy when she or he strikes up a conversation with you at the computer terminal, at your study room door, or in a chat room!

Knowledge and the academic library are organized by disciplines. When resources are published, they are given subject descriptions and call numbers by librarians of Congress according to the different disciplines (*http://cip.loc.gov/*). Library of Congress Subject Headings and Call Numbers help you see this organization in broad terms and in very specific terms (*http://www.loc.gov/catdir/cpso/lcco/lcco.html*). This very detailed classification system is a model of **excellence** that is used not only in the United States, but throughout the world. *But, what does this mean to you?* It means that books or e-Books have Library of Congress (LC) Call Numbers and Subject Headings and this little bit of information can tell you if the book you are using is a history book (D, E, F) or a social sciences book (H). Just knowing something about the way materials are put into the catalog (card catalog or online catalog) helps you know if you are being consistent in selecting resources for your courses' papers.

Another area to grasp an important research clue is in the area known as *Periodicals,* in other words, literature that comes out daily, weekly, monthly, quarterly, and sometimes annually. The major periodicals formats are magazines, journals and newspapers. Popular magazines have glossy photos, many ads, and short articles, which do not normally include bibliographies. Scholarly journals have few photos, more charts and graphs, if scientific in nature, few ads, and medium to long articles. The articles definitely include bibliographies (record of the scholarship) and in-text citations and/or footnotes throughout. Newspapers and their articles do not usually present the confusion that magazines and journals do; assignments calling for newspaper articles are usually straightforward. The following chart, prepared by UCF Library librarians, is very helpful in sorting through the maze of which periodicals format is right for you (*http://library.ucf.edu/Ask/scholarly.htm*).

Finally, *Information Literacy* is a buzzword that describes the awareness that there is an overwhelming quantity of information available these days, some of quality and some of questionable quality. This awareness is coupled with the recognition that the knowledge base in any given discipline grows very slowly. Basically, it follows then that a set of principles and strategies is needed to help locate, access, select, and then use information effectively and legally to accomplish a purpose. **Excellence** in your academic and your future professional life depends on how information literate you become. The American Library Association and the Association of Colleges and Research Libraries have responded to the information overload crisis and the need for a plan of action to deal with separating the "wheat from the chaff" (*http://www.ala.org/ala/acrl/acrlstandards/informationliteracycompetency.htm*).

In closing, whether you may walk in to the reference area of a library or whether you email, phone, IM, or fax your librarian, you are strongly advised to have a conversation with a librarian. Also, take advantage of as many self-paced tutorials that are available that help you navigate through the library world in print and online. When you begin to use a new resource, investigate its features. If it is a book, turn to the table of contents and the index. Notice what kind of organization has been imposed on the information, when it was published, and who wrote or edited it. If it is an online resource, click on the help pages and the dates of coverage of the information available for searching. Learn the Boolean Logic and other symbols that the database uses in order to combine search terms or exclude search terms. And don't, I repeat don't just choose articles that happen to be in full-text online! Read the abstracts of the search results and base your decision on an article's value or its relevance to your research topic, not whether it is available online in full-text. Leave plenty of time for requesting articles or books from the physical library or from Interlibrary Loan. Your authentic pursuit of **excellence** is at stake.

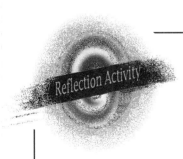

*Reflection Activity*

### View E-Literate Video

1. Go to: *http://www.kn.pacbell.com/media/ucla2.html*

2. Comment on the information presented in the E-Literate video (2001).

3. Post on the class message board whether you agree or disagree with the statement that in today's society the person without computer skills to access information and the critical thinking skills to evaluate the information "will be left behind?"

### *Take an Online Library Orientation*

1. Go to: *http://www.saintleo.edu/library*

2. Click on "Library Tutorial" and select "Library Orientation for Students" at *http://www.saintleo.edu/SaintLeo/Templates/Inner.aspx?pid=5129*

3. Read the first two parts of "The Internet" section of Saint Leo's Library Tutorial and take the practice quizzes on Search Engines and Evaluating Online Sources ("on the Internet").

4. Practice accessing the library electronic resources that are delivered "via the Internet;" these are also known as subscription online databases. Your Saint Leo webmail account information is your logon and password. If you are unsure of how to login, view the flash demo at *http://199.44.215.100/login_demo.htm*

### *On the Internet*

1. Go to: *http://searchenginewatch.com*

2. Go to Google's latest development at: *http://searchenginewatch.com/searchday/article.php/3437471*

3. Visit the Forum thread that is discussing this new service at *http://forums.searchenginewatch.com/showthread.php?threadid=2812*

4. Go to Google Scholar *http://scholar.google.com/* and post your comments on the results you get for a search.

5. Here are a few **Sample Databases "Via the Internet"**
   Ebsco         *http://www.epnet.com/academic/default.asp*
   ProQuest     *http://www.il.proquest.com/proquest/*
   Wilson        *http://www.hwwilson.com/Databases/omnifile.htm*

   **Boolean Search Tips—Lake Sumter Community College**

   *http://www.lscc.cc.fl.us/library/guides/boolsea.htm*

## PRACTICAL TIPS FOR USING THE LIBRARY AND INTERNET

A. Set up alerts in the databases for new articles that are posted on your research topic—alerts are email messages from the vendors like Ebsco and ProQuest that tell you an article has been added to the database with subject headings that match a description you provided of your research interests. Go to *http://www.il .proquest.com/division/pqnext/previews/alerts/setup.html http://faculty.valencia.cc.fl.us/infolit/EBSCO/saved_searches_alerts.htm* for more information, or simply ask a librarian!

B. Join a listserv of a scholarly association—ask your professor for the name and the website of an association that is linked with the discipline of your course. The association no doubt has a listserv to which you may subscribe and receive email messages from scholars asking each other questions in a particular field. For instance, Library Science's national association is ALA. Within ALA, there are many different library groups like public, school or special libraries. College Libraries usually subscribe to listservs that have academic library missions and therefore academic library discussions. One such listserv is DIGREF—for the librarians who want to share information with each other about digital reference.

C. Subscribe to a journal in your major field or read it at the library or online once a month or quarterly, whatever its publication frequency. See Ulrich's Periodical Listing at *http://www.ulrichsweb.com/ulrichsweb/*
See MLA Periodical Listing in Ebsco.

D. Attend a scholarly conference and attend presentations. Based on the new information you hear and the new authors you meet, ask a librarian to order new books (or e-Books) for the library's collection.

E. Write a paper with a faculty member and try using Interlibrary Loan Service to order books and articles from other libraries' collections if you do not find them at your own library or "cybrary." See *http://www.saintleo.edu/library* and click on "Interlibrary Loan and Document Delivery."

*Early drawing of Leo the Lion*
From Saint Leo Abbey Archives

**Is it history or hearsay?**

Saint Leo used to have a "real" lion as its official mascot.

**It's history**. A "real" lion was the official mascot years ago under the presidency of Dr. Southard in the 1970s. Its cage was located behind DeChantal Hall.

It is a **fusion** of the entire community that provides for an effective college life experience where you can become more aware of your own values and begin to examine and live these values. Educators Chickering & Gamson identified *Seven Principles of Good Practice* from which you can build on your values. They are as follows:

1. Get to know a faculty member.
2. Work with other students to attain your goals.
3. Talk about what you are learning with others.
4. Reflect on your own learning.
5. Use your time wisely.
6. Set high, yet realistic expectations for yourself.
7. Learn to respect and value different ways of learning.

*Source: Chickering and Gamson (1987).*

"It takes a whole community to educate a student."

—*George Kuh 2003*

**Reflection Activity**

### Seven Principles of Good Practice

1. Which of the seven principles do you follow?

2. Rank the seven principles from most important to least important.
   7 = most important,
   1 = least important

3. Choose two core values that you think are instrumental in following the seven principles. The values are: excellence, community, respect, personal development, responsible stewardship, and integrity.

## Reflection Questions

1. Why is it a good idea to integrate values outside of the online classroom?

2. What are some ways values can be integrated outside of online learning?

**Is it history or hearsay?**

In the 1960s, the college, like many others across the country, was the place of occasional "panty raids," where male students would sneak into the girls' dormitories and stealthily raid the female co-eds' underwear drawers. Unfortunately, for one unlucky student, his raid ended unexpectedly when, rummaging through drawers, he came face to face with one of the priory nuns.

***It's history.*** In the fall of 1959, 61 males and six females were admitted to Saint Leo. The college wasn't immune to the 1960s phenomena of panty raids. This particular incident ended abruptly when one nun investigated a noise coming from the girls' dormitories located on the floor above the nuns' living quarters.

**Is it history or hearsay?**

Over the years several students walking the campus in the quiet of late night have reported seeing a lone figure crossing by a window on the third floor of Saint Edward Hall, once a boy's residence hall. When they have entered the building or reported the sighting, no one was ever found.

***It's hearsay.*** Over the years, this same mysterious figure has been spotted crossing the same windows on the third floor of the building. Each time someone has investigated, no one has ever been found in the building.

"A learning community is where expectations are clear and the culture is distinctive; members are committed to being and remain open to changing and growing; where participants are present to each other in a web of truth-seeking and pursue a balanced, whole learning agenda in a milieu of welcome and belonging."

—*Carney Strange 2000*

Let's take a few minutes to complete the following activity.

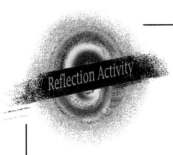

### Let's Match

### Directions

Match the core value with the appropriate actions by writing the first letter of the value next to the numbered item. You may use a core value more than once.

1. Being friendly to others

2. Community Service Day

3. Recycling programs

4. Doing the best you can everyday

5. Using appropriate internet netiquette

6. Turning in assignments

7. Learning about time and stress management

8. Doing your own academic work

9. Telling the truth at all times

10. Learning to be financially responsible

**E**xcellence

**C**ommunity

**R**espect

**P**ersonal Development

**R**esponsible Stewardship

**I**ntegrity

**Is it history or hearsay?**

Sunday mass used to be held outside of Saint Edward Hall for all students.

*It's history*. Tim Crosby, former student and now the tennis coach for Saint Leo, described one Sunday morning when two male students living on the first floor of Saint Edward Hall overslept and forgot to close their blinds the night before. They awoke to the entire student body right outside their windows.

*Prep school dorm room*
From Saint Leo Abbey Archives

**Is it history or hearsay?**

The first student to be expelled forged a check in order to attend the college.

*It's history*. A fifteen-year-old boy from Buffalo, New York forged a $90.00 check from his father to attend Saint Leo Military College.

Reflection Activity

### Ten-Minute Chat

### Directions

Chat about one of the two items below using the class discussion board.

1. Imagine that you are waiting to get into heaven. In order to get in, you are going to be judged on whether or not you have accomplished what you wanted to do during your university experience. How did you do? For the most part, did you stay on track? Which values did you include in your lifestyle?

2. Imagine that you have received a million dollars. What would you now do with your life? How would values influence your new lifestyle?

**Is it history or hearsay?**

Head tennis coach, Tim Crosby, has been on campus for the administration of eight Saint Leo presidents.

***Although it seems incredible,*** Tim Crosby began as a student in the 1960s and then joined the faculty upon graduation. Thus, he has either been a student or a faculty member under the following presidents:
Father Stephen Hermann, O.S.B. (1961–1968),
Dr. Anthony W. Zaitz (1968–1971),
Dr. Thomas Southard (1971–1985),
Dr. Daniel Henry (1985–1987),
Monsignor Frank M. Mouch (1987–1997),
Dr. Arthur F. Kirk, Jr. (1997–Present).

*1938 school bus*
From Saint Leo Abbey Archives

## REFLECTION QUESTIONS

1. Why is it important for a leader to have values?

2. What values do you think are important for a leader?

3. What is it that you most like about your experience as an online learner?

4. What do people need most from others?




5. How will the core values help you meet these needs?

**Is it history or hearsay?**

Guess the order in which the buildings were built from earliest to the most recent. Then look at the bottom of page for historical reporting of construction.

_____ Abbey Church

_____ Crawford Hall

_____ Julia Deal Lewis Hall

_____ Library

_____ Marion Bowman Activities Center

_____ McDonald Activities Center

_____ Saint Edward Hall

_____ Saint Francis Hall

_____ Saint Leo Hall/Abbey

*It's history* only if you guessed correctly! See answers provided.

**Answers:** Saint Leo Hall/Abbey = 1906, Saint Edward Hall = 1926, Abbey Church = begun in 1936 and completed in 1948, Saint Francis Hall = 1952, Library = 1958 (remodeled in 1986), Crawford Hall = 1961, McDonald Activities Center = 1962 (remodeled in 2003), Julia Deal Lewis Hall = 1967, Marion Bowman Activities Center = 1970.

*Reflection Activity*

### Which Value Is It?

### Directions

Rank order the importance of each value as it relates to the questions.

1 = Highest and/or most important value

6 = Lowest and/or least important value

1. Which value is most important in developing positive relationships?

   _____ Community          _____ Integrity          _____ Responsible Stewardship

   _____ Respect            _____ Excellence         _____ Personal Development

2. Which value is most important in facing the issue of racism in our society?

   _____ Community          _____ Integrity          _____ Responsible Stewardship

   _____ Respect            _____ Excellence         _____ Personal Development

3. Which value is most important in facing the issue of preserving natural resources?

   _____ Community          _____ Integrity          _____ Responsible Stewardship

   _____ Respect            _____ Excellence         _____ Personal Development

4. Which value is most important in being a responsible and mature adult?

   _____ Community          _____ Integrity          _____ Responsible Stewardship

   _____ Respect            _____ Excellence         _____ Personal Development

5. Which value is most important in being a positive role model for others?

   _____ Community          _____ Integrity          _____ Responsible Stewardship

   _____ Respect            _____ Excellence         _____ Personal Development

6. Which value is important to you when dealing with a personal crisis in your life?

   _____ Community          _____ Integrity          _____ Responsible Stewardship

   _____ Respect            _____ Excellence         _____ Personal Development

7. Which value would you most want to share with your children and why?

   _____ Community          _____ Integrity          _____ Responsible Stewardship

   _____ Respect            _____ Excellence         _____ Personal Development

Wrap-Up: Discuss why you rank ordered the items in the order you chose.

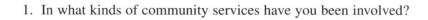

## REFLECTION QUESTIONS

1. In what kinds of community services have you been involved?

2. How does this service enhance your personal development?

# ACTIVITIES FOR INTEGRATING VALUES FOR ONLINE LEARNERS

*As you begin the activities portion of the book, your instructor may encourage you to complete the activities through chat, message board postings, or asynchronous assignments. See your instructor's directions as you go along.*

*EXCELLENCE*

*COMMUNITY*

*RESPECT*

*PERSONAL DEVELOPMENT*

*RESPONSIBLE STEWARDSHIP*

*INTEGRITY*

# CHAPTER 4

# EXCELLENCE

*Look for your instructor's directions to complete the activities.*

*Excellence seems to be an easy concept to understand at first glance. But look in a dictionary, and you'll find a long line of synonyms that shows just how differently people see this sometimes-elusive value. Graciousness, grandeur, accomplishment, sophistication, preeminence, supremacy, transcendence, and even perfection all compete for meaning. What does excellence mean to you?*

> "Excellence is the gradual result of always striving to do better."
> —*Pat Riley*

> "Excellence is rarely found, more rarely valued."
> —*Johann Wolfgang von Goethe*

> "There are no speed limits on the road to excellence."
> —*David W. Johnson*

## REFLECTION QUESTIONS

1. What does it mean to you to be a student of **excellence?**

2. Identify three people who have led a life of **excellence.**

3. What ways have you identified for yourself to lead you on the path to **excellence?**

### Memory Skills and Excellence

An **excellent** memory is only a part of being an **excellent** student.

1. Preview the following site from Virginia Technical Institute: http://www.ucc.vt.edu/stdysk/remember.html.

2. Review the list of hints to increase your memory skills.

3. Choose the five most important hints.

4. Which hints seem most applicable to you in chemistry course? In history? Writing?

### How Do You Generate Interest in a Topic?

A good memory depends in part on how willing you are to invest time and effort in learning the skills of memory. *But, what happens when you are not interested in a subject?*

1. Go to the following website: http://www.mtsu.edu/~studskl/mem.html.

2. Share why you think interest is such an issue in memory.

3. How can you generate interest in a subject or an assignment if you have none?

4. How are interest and **excellence** related?

5. Can you gain **excellence** in an area and not be interested? Why or why not?

**How much is it without the tradition of excellence?**

*From www.CartoonStock.com*

## MATHEMATICS

Opportunities to demonstrate your knowledge of algebraic concepts and problem-solving skills are encouraged in mathematics. A pursuit of **excellence** in beginning level courses will enhance your analytical skills and personal interests.

## How Do I Count the Ways . . . Accurately?

Discovery learning is a type of inquiry-based learning method that is often used in problem-solving scenarios so that you, as the learner, can draw on your own experiences and prior knowledge to 'discover' appropriate concepts. This active learning process encourages you to strive for **excellence** as you are challenged to go beyond textbook examples in solving realistic problems. In this way, you formulate responses based on the data and develop your own strategies to accurately process the information. You have the unique opportunity to use your intuition, be creative, and develop lifelong learning skills. An example is given below.

### Scenario

You have just been hired as the new office manager for The McClure Company, Inc. of Desoto Plaza. You have the responsibility to determine the tax payment for the company for all tenants for the month of June. You will submit a check to the Department of Revenue covering the 7% state sales tax for all tenants. Desoto Physical Therapy is exempt from state tax as a health organization. Eckerd Drugs pays its own tax to the state and therefore does not submit any taxes to the Desoto property owners.

### Directions

1. Place an *X* next to the companies that are tax exempt.

2. Calculate and total the columns below keeping in mind that 2-1/2% of the total tax owed or a maximum of $30 may be deducted from the tax bill each month.

3. Fill out the check appropriately.

4. Answer the questions that follow.

## JUNE FINANCIAL SUMMARY

| Status Tenant | Gross | Gross-Sales | Tax |
|---|---|---|---|
| ABC Ceramics | 577.26 | | |
| Bealls Outlet | 3,566.66 | | |
| Carmike Cinema | 1,471.25 | | |
| Desoto Physical Therapy | 4,738.01 | | |
| Dollar General | 2,172.63 | | |
| Eckerd Drugs | 2,333.34 | | |
| H&R Block | 458.77 | | |

| Status Tenant | Gross | Gross-Sales | Tax |
|---|---|---|---|
| Jim's Fashions | 1,551.51 | | |
| Merle Norman | 567.40 | | |
| Renter's Choice | 1,924.99 | | |
| S.C. Insurance | 423.59 | | |
| Save-A-Lot | 4,458.33 | | |
| Sun Title | 1,070.00 | | |
| Superstar Video | 817.99 | | |
| **Total:** | **$26,131.73** | | |
| | | Subtotal: | |
| | | Deductions: | |
| | | Total Tax Due: | |

1. What steps did you take to ensure you modeled **excellence** in finding the total tax payment for the McClure Company?

2. What would be the consequences for not following the steps accurately?

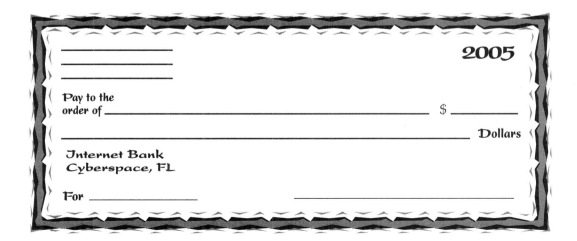

Reflection Activity

### *Math in the Real World*

The difference between rote learning and real world application in math is the challenge of **excellence.** It is easy to plug in a formula and write in narrative form, but true **excellence** focuses on finding real world applications that show how deeply you understand the mathematical concepts and formulas. This activity explores linear equations as they relate to the real world.

Let's say that you are planning on taking a road trip and you go on-line to search for competitive rates for rental cars. You see that Hertz charges $25.00 a day and 10 cents a mile, while Avis charges $5.00 a day and 50 cents a mile. You must now figure out which company actually has the better deal.

### *Directions*

1. Search online for current rates and reservations for Hertz and Avis.

2. Compare the two rental car rates by completing the chart below.

### RATES AND RESERVATIONS:

|  | Hertz | Avis |
| --- | --- | --- |
| Rental Date and Time: | | |
| Pick-up Date: | | |
| Car Class: | | |
| Car Type: | | |
| **Expenses:** | | |
| Per Day: | | |
| Per Mile: | | |
| Base Rate: | | |
| Other: | | |

3. Write your information as a simple linear model.

4. Post your model on the message board and respond to a classmate's model.

5. Post answers to three of the following on the message board.

   • What does the equation represent?

   • Why is it useful?

   • What is the dependent variable?

   • What does it represent in the context of the problem?

   • What is the independent variable?

   • What does it represent in the context of the problem?

   • What is the slope?

   • What does it represent in terms of the problem?

   • Why is the dependent variable dependent upon the independent variable?

   • What is the intercept for the dependent variable?

   • What does it represent in terms of the problem?

   • What are the domain and range?

   • What do they represent in the context of the problem?

6. Find particular values that are solutions to the equation and complete the following:

   • Describe the relationship between the dependent and independent variable.

   • Illustrate why the particular variables represent a solution to the equation.

### Solve This Riddle

The core value of **excellence** states that all of us, individually and collectively should strive towards being morally responsible leaders. In the ever-expanding field of mathematics, those who endeavor to solve these time-consuming problems through patient and earnest work in order to make the world a more understandable place are still pursuing solutions to age-old riddles.

### Directions

Read the following article and answer the questions that follow.

## Awaiting proof of solved riddle, math hero shies from publicity

MOSCOW—In his office overlooking the faded pastel mansions along a St. Petersburg, Russia, canal, a young mathematician spent eight solitary years grappling with the Poincare Conjecture, one of the most frustrating conundrums in math.

Now, colleagues say, Russian Grigori Perelman might not only have solved the century-old riddle. He might have helped advance many areas of math and physics and made it possible to better understand the shape of the universe.

If "Grisha" Perelman's proof of the Poincare is correct—and many mathematicians suspect it is—it will seal his transformation from an obscure researcher into one of the world's leading scientists.

And he will become the first person eligible to claim a $1-million prize offered by the Clay Mathematics Institute of Cambridge, Mass., for solving what it calls one of the seven central problems in math.

But the 37-year-old native of St. Petersburg doesn't seem interested in money or acclaim. While he could probably get a far more lucrative job in the West, he earns about $200 a month at the Steklov Institute of Mathematics in St. Petersburg. In 1996, he refused to accept an award in Budapest, Hungary, from the European Mathematical Society.

"In my opinion, any public discussion of my work at the moment is premature and counterproductive," he wrote in an e-mail to the *Baltimore Sun.*

Colleagues say Perelman is jealous of his privacy, and fearful attention would distract him from his work. He also might be concerned that prize money could make him a target of the Russian underworld.

"I think he wants to be a private person," said John Milnor, director of the Institute for Mathematical Science at the State University of New York at Stony Brook. "He doesn't want to be a media hero, where he can walk out without being recognized, where he has a fear for his life."

Partly, Perelman is probably leery of prematurely claiming victory. Dozens of researchers have tackled the Poincare Conjecture. It goes to the heart of topology, or the mathematical study of surfaces, which holds that the world consists of two basic shapes, the sphere and the doughnut. Poincare speculated, in effect, that certain rules governing these three-dimensional shapes also apply to the same shapes projected into four and more dimensions.

Two years ago, mathematician Martin Dunwoody of Southampton University in Britain caused a stir when he published a proposal proof. But Dunwoody, like his predecessors, was proved wrong.

Milnor cautioned that Perelman's proof could have hidden flaws. "It's been a puzzle and a challenge for 100 years," he said. "There have been many positive first steps and many false proofs. It's the kind of a subject where it's very easy to make a mistake if you're not careful."

Experts say it could take six months to a year to verify Perelman's work, which is being scrutinized by teams around the world. But the work appears to have avoided the pitfalls of past efforts. Colleagues say even if his proof has hidden flaws, it represents a major advance in math.

"Although at the moment it is still too soon to declare a definitive solution to the problem, Perelman's ideas are highly original and of deep insight," wrote Michael Anderson of Stony Brook in a recent issue of *Notices of the American Mathematical Society.*

**—Read Perelman's theories at www.arxiv.org/abs/math.DG/0303109/.**

*From* The Baltimore Sun *by Douglas Birch. Copyright © 2004, The Baltimore Sun. Reprinted by permission.*

1. How long has Perelman been working with the Poincare Conjecture?

2. What is the Poincare Conjecture?

3. If proven correct, what would be the benefits to the field of mathematics? How would Perelman benefit?

4. How would you characterize Perelman? Support your answer with details from the article.

5. How would you compare Perelman and his work to the core value of **excellence?**

# PHILOSOPHY/RELIGION

### Calling All Angels

In the aftermath of the September 11 tragedy, our fears and anxieties for the future have been expressed in a variety of ways, music being one such mode. It is also not uncommon during times of need that people seek a higher being to help them understand the events that have taken place as they search for answers.

### Directions

Read the lyrics from the song *Calling All Angels* by Train. This song can be found in its entirety through a search at http://www.lyricsondemand.com

## REFLECTION QUESTIONS

1. What are your thoughts after reading these lyrics? What is the author trying to say?

2. The chorus for this song uses the repetitive phrase '*I won't give up, if you don't give up.*' What does that mean to you?

3. The core value of **excellence** states that we should become morally responsible leaders. How would you describe a morally responsible leader in today's post-September 11 climate?

## *A Picture Is Worth a Thousand Words*

Imagine that you and a loved one are strolling through a local art festival. All of a sudden you see a booth filled with pictures, drawings, oil paintings, photos, and lots of modern art. There are sports photos, family portraits, war scenes, and many contemporary pieces; yet, one picture in particular catches your eye. It is of a small town filled with young people dancing in the streets. You pause and begin to wonder more about this scene and quietly ask yourself, *who are they? how come they are in a big group? why are they all smiling? when did this take place? where did . . .* but, with a slight tug of your arm, you continue on to the next booth.

This brief moment caused you to *reflect* on something of interest to you or to say it another way; you acted on your values. Maybe it was the faces, the poses, the colors, the setting, whatever the case, you were motivated to stop and ponder over the scene. This process, called reflection, is precisely how the university values are presented to you. Values are not directly taught, but they are presented for you to consider and connect to in your life. It is this process that also encourages you to strive for **excellence.**

## REFLECTION QUESTIONS

1. How do values fit into your life?

2. Do you study them? read about values? listen to or watch others?

## Hey You, Listen!

You might want to refer back to the section titled "The Benedictine Heritage" in Chapter 1 in completing this section.

The very first word in the Rule of Saint Benedict is "Listen."

"Listen . . . with the ear of your heart."
*RB Prologue*

1. Why do you think it is significant for Benedict to begin in this way?

The Rule consists of a prologue and 73 chapters all written in less than 100 pages. The final chapter says "Now, we have written this Rule that, observing it in monasteries, we may show that we have acquired at least some moral righteousness, or a beginning of the monastic life" (RB73).

## REFLECTION QUESTIONS

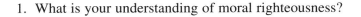

1. What is your understanding of moral righteousness?

2. How does this relate to **excellence?**

### *Balance, Coordinate, Harmonize*

The Rule of Saint Benedict calls for study, work, and prayer. Saint Benedict recognized the importance of balancing physical, emotional, intellectual, and spiritual needs. Today this might seem challenging and maybe even impossible with competition from work, family, class assignments, and your own social life.

## REFLECTION QUESTIONS

On your own, reflect on the following questions.

1. How do you balance your daily life?

2. Do you strive to do your best? Do you set goals for yourself?

3. If so, how? If you don't set goals, how do you know if you are successful?

4. Now working with a classmate, state a goal for a class and your plans to achieve it.

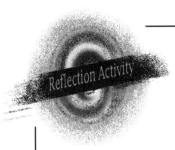

### *Learn to Read or Read to Learn?*

Saint Benedict asked his monks to first learn to read so that they could memorize psalms for common prayer. Then he asked them to read to learn in order to practice and carry out what they read.

*Lectio Divina* is reading or studying time for monks. Just as you read and perhaps re-read your notes or text chapters before an exam, monks read and re-read Scriptures daily. Studying, along with prayer and work, is a hallmark of the Rule.

### REFLECTION QUESTIONS

1. What are your study habits? List them below.

2. Post your top five study habits on the class discussion board.

3. Compare your habits to another classmate's by completing the Venn diagram below.

4. What did you discover?

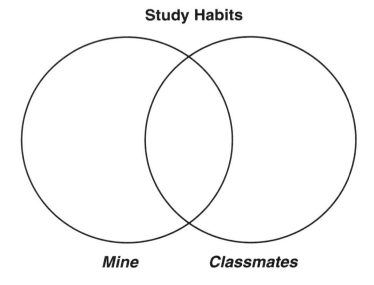

**Study Habits**

*Mine*          *Classmates*

### *Internet Connections to the Rule of Saint Benedict*

Visit one of the following websites and read about the history of Saint Benedict and his Rule. Then, with a classmate, answer the following questions:

### *Websites:*

The Rule of Saint Benedict

http://www.osb.org/rb/

Catholic Encyclopedia—The Rule of Saint Benedict:

http://www.newadvent.org/cathen/02436a.htm

About the Rule of Saint Benedict by Abbot Primate Jerome Theisen, O.S.B.

http://www.osb.org/gen/rule.html

Medieval Source Book—The Rule of Saint Benedict, c. 530

http://www.fordham.edu/halsall/source/rul-benedict.html

The Holy Rule of Saint Benedict

http://www.christdesert.org/noframes/holyrule/holyrule_home.html

The Holy Rule of Saint Benedict, 1949 Edition, translated by Rev. Boniface Verheyen, O.S.B., of St. Benedict's Abbey, Atchison, Kansas

http://www.ccel.org/b/benedict/rule2/rule.html

### REFLECTION QUESTIONS

1. Predict what Saint Benedict would say about online learning today.

2. Compare the values of the Rule with your university mission and values.

# THE COMMON GOOD AND THE RULE OF SAINT BENEDICT

What is the "common good?" According to the Catechism of the Catholic Church "common good" is 'the sum total of social conditions which allow people either as groups or as individuals to reach their fulfillment more fully and more easily' (par. 1906). "The common good concerns the life of all." It implies that what is good for one must be good for all. As a human being, you are part of a whole community. Realizing that the whole is greater than any of its parts is the essence of undertaking the importance of the common good. For this reason, the common good is valued more than that of each individual. This concept applies not just to the physical needs but also to the dignity, emotional state, and spiritual growth of a community and/or society.

Saint Benedict explains, "No one is to pursue what he judges better for himself, but instead, what he judges better for someone else" (RB 72:7). Therefore, in a society where individualism dominates, it is often a challenge to work toward the common good. *Listening* to one another is a good start. According to the Rule of Saint Benedict listening is very important because we each have insight, encouragement, wisdom, and/or talent to offer to each other. An individualist may ask, *What do I need for myself?* A person who values the common good may ask, *How do my particular wants and needs affect others?* Which question do YOU ask of yourself?

You may consider integrating a commitment to the common good and respect for each individual. Saint Benedict states that everyone has gifts from God. The challenge is to use personal gifts for the good of the community. You might ask yourself, *How can I best use God's gifts for the common good?* Saint Benedict stresses the importance of love and respect for each person regardless of social class, age, gender, religion, race, ethnicity, or other forms of marginalization. It is possible to reach out to others with care, respect, and love without diminishing your identity. Each individual can serve others for the good of all as the gifts you receive from God are not just for you, but for others as well. Neither human joy nor sorrow should be a matter of indifference to your community, because ultimately what affects one affects all. Some questions to ask yourself are: *How do my choices affect other people? What are the needs of others compared to my desires?*

*Reflection Activity*

### Choices and Consequences

Think of a time when your actions were based on the best interest of another student, friend, or family member.

   1. What were the consequences of your decision?

2. How did you feel afterward?

3. Were the consequences what you intended?

Now consider your future endeavors. Whatever they may be, you might want to include values into your spiritual and daily life. *How will you do this?* First, be aware of the consequences of your choices. There are different levels of complexity to your choices and these also affect the variety of consequences. Some choices are as simple as choosing to recycle. Others are more complex such as a decision as a CEO of a corporation, facing an ethical dilemma regarding hiring decisions and profitability.

A CEO of Levi Strauss in a branch office in Bangladesh developed a creative solution to an ethical dilemma related to whether or not to hire children under the age of 14. The CEO chose not to hire these children, but decided to pay the children wages while they attended school, providing them with books and school materials, then hired them after their 14th birthday. The decision was made knowing that the children, in most cases, are the breadwinners of the family.

4. How would you have handled this ethical dilemma?

5. Would you have hired children under the age of 14, which in Bangladesh is not considered unethical?

The families needed the money and you would be saving the company money by taking advantage of low-cost labor. On the other hand, *would you have looked into different alternatives in order to enable the children to attend school while being able to provide for their families?*

You will be constantly confronted with difficult situations in your lives that call for evaluation considering the common good. Priorities may need to be reordered so that the needs of many are satisfied instead of the desires of a few.

Questions may cross your mind while envisioning your future. *What does it all mean to me? Do I have goals that apply the common good in my life?* You are empowered to improve the lives of other human beings by using wisely the gifts given to you (i.e., intelligence, talents, knowledge, resources, etc.). Every gift carries a responsibility to use for the good of all in the community.

"Getcha spirit/mind
right."
—D-Team

*Fusing It All: A Philosophical Look at Values*

Using your class discussion board, discuss the following questions as they relate to becoming a morally responsible leader.

    1.  Overall, how does **excellence** fit into your online community?

2.  Explain how **excellence** and prioritizing values may help define specific philosophical groups.

3.  Name some common characteristics that can be found in two philosophical groups (conservative, liberal) that may appear on the surface to be contradictions? What values are characteristic of each group? Are there similarities? Is **excellence** always demonstrated?

4.  Identify the conflicts that may develop when trying to live a life of both **community** and **personal development.** Take a position as to which value should/should not take place over the other.

5.  Discuss two basic fallacies (errors in reasoning) of argument and how hiding behind arguments may help these fallacies. Post which core value(s), assisted you the most in defending your response.

# CHAPTER 5

# COMMUNITY

*Pssst . . .*

*Look for your instructor's directions to complete the activities.*

*The word community seems to have come into the English language in the 14th century from the Latin word **communitas**, meaning common. We use the term broadly these days to describe people who live in a common location or who are in a common situation, as in a retirement community. But the word suggests much more. A community is also a group of individuals united in a common purpose. In the Rule, community plays an integral part of the Benedictine life. Prior to Benedict's Rule, a monastic life meant a life of seclusion. But Benedict believed that a life of working and living with others brings us closer to God.*

### REFLECTION QUESTIONS

1. How do you balance being an individual and a contributing part of a **community?**

2. How can you build more of a sense of a **community** within your university as an online learner?

3. What is the **community** that you most identify with right now?

> "Without community, there is no liberation, only the most vulnerable and temporary armistice between an individual and her oppression. But community must not mean shedding our differences, nor the pathetic pretense that differences do not exist."
> —Audre Lorde

> "For a community to be whole and healthy, it must be based on people's love and concern for one another."
> —Millard Fuller

> "When we come together to play and be, we are truly ourselves. When we are truly ourselves it is wonderful and when we act collectively in that wonder, we do transformative work for our community and our world."
> —Brad Colby at Komo I

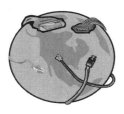

### *Active Learning and the Community*

Gardner & Jewler (2004) define active learning as "simply a method that involves students, or learners in an active manner. It takes place whenever your teacher asks you a question in class, puts you in groups to solve a problem, requires you to make an oral presentation to the class, or does anything else that gives you and other students a voice in the learning process" (49).

1. Explore the definitions of *active learning* at any of the following websites.

   - http://trc.ucdavis.edu/trc/ta/tatips/activelearning.pdf

   - http://honolulu.hawaii.edu/intranet/committees/FacDevCom/guidebk/teachtip/active.htm

   - http://www.ntlf.com/html/lib/bib/91-9dig.htm

2. Working with a small group of students, choose one person to e-mail your group's responses to the questions below to your instructor.

3. How do active learning and **community** play an influential role in your learning?

4. Is active learning different from lecture style classes? How do both provide for a **community** of learners?

5. Take a moment to reflect on this experience in collaborating with other students to complete a class assignment. How did it go? What made it successful? What would you do differently to make it more successful for everyone?

# FINE ARTS

**Reflection Activity**

## Double-Entry Journal

## Directions

Complete the double-entry journal below by choosing three excerpts from the song, *Where Is the Love* by the Black-Eyed Peas and writing them in the left-hand column. Then reflect on what they mean to you in the right-hand column. When writing your reflections, please relate them to the core values of **respect** and **community.** This song can be found in its entirety through a search at www.lyricsondemand.com. Post one of your quotes and reflections on the class discussion board.

| Quotes | Reflections |
|---|---|
| 1. | |
| 2. | |
| 3. | |

*Reflection Activity*

## Home Alone

## Directions

1. Read the article *Home Alone, With the Family.*

# Home alone, with the family

**Great rooms and open floor plans give way to alcoves and getaway rooms as families opt for more privacy.**

By June Fletcher
Wall Street Journal

Carl and Tiffany Ledbetter like to spend time at home together—just not necessarily in the same room. So they built a 3,600-square foot house with special rooms for studying and sewing, separate sitting areas for each child, and a master bedroom far from both. Then there's the "escape room," where "any family member can go to get away from the rest of us," Carl Ledbetter says.

The Mercer Island, Wash., industrial designer says his 7- and 11-year-old daughters fight less, because their new house gives them so many ways to avoid each other. "It just doesn't make sense for us to do everything together all the time," he says.

After two decades of pushing the open floor plan—where domestic life revolved around a big central space and exposed kitchens gave everyone a view of half the house—major builders and top architects are walling people off. They're touting one-person "Internet alcoves," locked-door "away rooms" and his-and-her offices on opposite ends of the house.

The new floor plans offer so much seclusion, they're "good for the dysfunctional family," says Gopal Ahluwahlia, director of research for the National Association of Home Builders.

At the International Builders Show in Las Vegas earlier this year, the showcase "Ultimate Family Home" hardly had a family room. It was broken up into a media center and separate "home management center," which itself was divided by a countertop. The boy's personal playroom had its own 42-inch plasma TV, and the girl's bedroom had a secret mirrored door leading to a "hideaway karaoke room." There was even a separate room under the stairs for the family dog.

"We call this the ultimate home for families who don't want anything to do with one another," says Mike McGee, chief executive of Pardee Homes of Los Angeles, builder of the model.

Designers say the new antisocial architecture is partly a backlash against the enforced camaraderie of the residential layouts of the '80s and '90s, with their "great rooms" and shared spaces that made it tough to get away from it all (and tougher to hide messes from guests).

That form of architecture, which initially became popular in Southern California, really took off around the country when building costs began soaring. Architects saw it not only as a novelty, but a way to save money on construction.

Urban theorist James Howard Kunstler, author of *The Geography of Nowhere* and other books on suburbia, says the big open plans and communal designs run counter to a traditional sign of status, the ability to keep others out. "Privacy is the ultimate luxury," he says.

The new closed-door policy, some designers say, also appeals to the growing number of people who marry and have children later, and who are accustomed to having time to themselves. Don Evans, an Orlando architect, says he is drawing up plans more often for America's blended families. "He might be in his 50s, she might be in her 30s, and the kids could range from very young to teenagers—people want walls today," he says. "You need separate spaces to stay married."

The extra rooms don't necessarily mean extra room. After four decades of annual increases in the size of the average new U.S. home, it has remained steady at around 2,320 square feet for the past three years. The difference is that living rooms and other common spaces are shrinking and small rooms are multiplying.

The National Association of Home Builders, the builder's trade group, estimates that the average U.S. living room has been squeezed to only three-quarters the size it was a decade ago. The latest U.S. Census figures show that the average household size dropped 2 percent, to 2.59 people, in the decade ended in 2000.

At the same time, the number of new-home buyers demanding at least four bedrooms is up 7 percent since 1990. In many cases, buyers turn the extra bedrooms into closed-off refuges for pursuits like Pilates and coin collecting.

For Larry and Susan Caruthers, a room of one's own—plus a getaway from that one—was so important they rejected 300 houses before paying $741,000 last October for a colonial in Ashburn, Va. The 4,000-square-foot home has a "retreat" room off the master bedroom, where Larry watches television, and a nook in the dressing area dedicated to Susan's sewing. The four-bedroom home also has separate bathrooms for each of the two grown Caruthers children when they visit. "We all need a little down time from each other," says Mrs. Caruthers, a 51-year-old homemaker.

In their new house, Michael Coffey, a Hatfield, Mass., furniture sculptor and his wife, a university archivist, have an office apiece, each on a different floor, plus five patios and two decks. It's a lot better than their old house, where they shared an office and his messiness and her neatness caused tensions. Coffey says being able to shut the door is one of the secrets of familial happiness. "We like our own space, our privacy, our own rooms," he says. "Everyone should have a room of one's own."

The blueprints for these fortresses of solitude are being drawn up by both mass-market developers and high-end architects. In one of its newer plans, Toll Brothers of Huntington Valley, Pa., offers a room off the master bedroom that can be closed off with double doors. For a further retreat from the master bedroom, there's a "princess suite" with its own walk-in closet and bathroom. Greystone Homes, a division of Miami-based Lennar Corp., offers a master-bedroom retreat, plus separate study and library areas.

Cambridge, Mass., architect Graham Gund says some clients are now asking for movable walls so they can close off rooms. Evans, the Orlando architect, recently designed a nearly 7,000-square-foot home with two Internet alcoves (one upstairs, one down) and a family room that's divided into a "gathering area" for talking and a "leisure" area for a pool table and other games. Upstairs, each of five guest suites has its own sitting area, and there are two separate play areas.

The approach isn't for all architects. William Sherman, chairman of the department of architecture and landscape architecture at the University of Virginia, says all the cutup spaces make families more isolated and lonelier than ever. "People don't even gather in the same spot to watch TV anymore, Sherman says. "It's sad."

2. What is your reaction to the direction that the architecture is taking?

3. Where in your house do you spend the most time and why?

4. What is your reaction to the quote, "We call this the ultimate home for families who don't want anything to do with one another."

5. Create an architectural design for your ideal house. How would you describe your house? Is it community-oriented or individual-oriented?

*Use this space to create your ideal house.*

# PHILOSOPHY/RELIGION

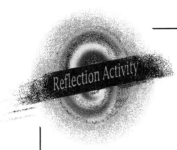

### *What's a Community?*

A community includes respect, stewardship, cooperation, sincerity, trust, openness, hospitality, support, and. . . .

1. Add characteristics to the description above that accurately portray your **community.**

2. What makes an online **community** meaningful? moral?

*Reflection Activity*

### Values?

Father Michael Pacella III shares, "Values that are void of truth have no historical grounding and lack spirituality."

    1. Do you agree with this statement? Defend your response.

Father Pacella continues to say . . . "For instance, in Christian morality, talking about blushing may lead to a scientific perspective, sociological perspective, and then to a spiritual perspective grounding it in Scripture. Discussion leads to collective (community) conscience and the call to accountability."

Think about another topic on Christian morality and discuss its applicability to the scientific, sociological, and spiritual perspectives. Are there other fields of study or academic communities that this topic may fit into as well? How do values fit in?

Pacella continues . . . "There is usually a moral consensus that there are certain moral expectations that we have of each other regardless of our religious affiliation or training. For instance, you do not expect your peers to steal from you. You do not inquire as to their religious affiliations, it is simply a moral expectation born out of commonly held values."

    1. Are we born with innate values? If yes, list the values. If no, explain.

    2. Can values be taught? Why or why not?

Post a moral expectation that you have of yourself. Do you have the same moral expectations of your friends? Why or why not?

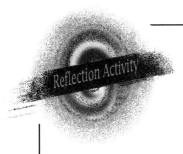

### Values: What Do They Mean to Me?

Professor Carney Strange and Father Harry Hagan, list the following foundational values in which to build a Benedictine community. Take a moment and reflect on each one based on your expectations and experiences as an online learner.

1. *Traditio et Regula* (Tradition and Rule)
   The focus of a community is placed on customs (tradition) and written documents (rule) to create an overall identity and values structure.

   a. Briefly describe the rules, customs, and traditions at your university.

   b. What makes your university distinct from others?

   c. Do the rules and traditions fit your needs? If so, explain.

2. *Stabilitas* (Stability)
   Every person has a commitment to the community endured through pride, stewardship, and personal ownership.

   a. What is your commitment to your major? your friends? your spouse? your university?

   b. What supports your commitment?

c. Describe your overall sense of pride and stewardship to your college experience.

3. *Conversatio* (Openness to Change and Grow)
   This value suggests being open to learning from others. Humility and a commitment to truth are essential virtues in changing and growing.

   a. In what ways do you resist change?

   b. Are you willing to take risks?

4. *Ora et Labora* (Prayer and Work)

   a. Do you take time for yourself?

   b. How do you see yourself living a balanced life during your four years of college? After college?

5. *Obedientia* (Obedience through Listening)

   a. Do you listen to others? peers? professors? advisors? coworkers? family members? etc.

   b. Is it sometimes challenging to listen? Why or why not?

6. *Hospitalitas* (Hospitality Is Being Open to Others)

   a. How do you handle interruptions?

   b. How do you demonstrate a sense of caring for others?

# HISTORY

Two core values that tie into American History are **respect** and **community.** Read the Saint Leo University definitions of these two values below.

**Respect**—Animated in the spirit of Jesus Christ, we value all individuals' unique talents, respect their dignity and strive to foster their commitment to excellence in our work. Our community's strength depends on the unity and diversity of our people, on the free exchange of ideas and on learning, living, and working harmoniously.

**Community**—Saint Leo University develops hospitable Christian learning communities everywhere we serve. We foster a spirit of belonging, unity, and interdependence based on mutual trust and respect to create socially responsible environments that challenge all of us to listen, to learn, to change, and to serve.

Using your knowledge of the many events that have taken place in our history and the core values of **respect** and **community,** complete the Think–Pair–Share activity.

### Think–Pair–Share

1. Think about the following question: Why do you suppose that the two core values of **respect** and **community** may be integrated in an American History course? Write your comments below.

2. Post your response to question one to the class discussion board.

3. Reply to another student's response.

*Source: Kagan, S. (1994).* Cooperative learning. *San Juan Capistrano, CA: Kagan Cooperative Learning.*

### *The Great Depression*

Quickwrite: In five minutes, write as much as you can about the Great Depression.

Read the quote below.

*Unable to pay mortgages or rent, many families lived off the generosity of forgiving landlords. Some traded down to smaller quarters or simply lost their homes. In a single day in April 1931, an estimated one-fourth of Mississippi went to auction. By 1932 between 1 million and 2 million Americans were homeless wanderers, among them an estimated 25,000 nomadic families (Davidson, et al., p. 690).*

1. The core value of **community** emphasizes a spirit of belonging, unity, and interdependence. What effect do you feel the Great Depression had on this sense of **community?**

### Open-Mind Portrait

*Mother and two children on the road, Tulelake, Siskiyou County, California, 1939.*

From Library of Congress, Prints and Photographs Division, FSA/OWI Collection.

Take a close look at the photograph above, especially the woman's face. This photograph was taken during the time of the Great Depression. This was a time of great hardship and humiliation for most families where many lost their jobs, homes, and a sense of community.

Create an open-mind portrait of this woman by writing inside the outline of her head what thoughts she might have been thinking as this picture was taken.

### Room in a Tenement, 1910

According to Merriam-Webster, a tenement is an apartment building "barely meeting minimum standards of sanitation, safety, and comfort for housing poorer families" (p. 945).

Examine the picture *Room in a tenement, 1910* below. Then answer the following questions:

1. How many people are in this room?

2. How would you describe the conditions of this one-room home?

3. Look closely at each person's facial expression. What do you see?

4. What kinds of activities do you think take place in this room?

5. How does this image tell you about urban life around the turn of the century?

6. What sense of community do you see taking place in these tenement houses?

Jacob A. Riis Collection, Room in a tenement, 1910. Museum of The City of New York.

# PSYCHOLOGY

## *Working with Others*

The university **community** is no different than the professional **community** served by psychologists. As such, it is important that we identify, acknowledge, and respect the values and beliefs of others, even if we do not completely agree with their feelings. The core values of **respect** and **community** both task us with the responsibility of appreciating others for who they are as well as coming together with those around us, irrespective of background or personal beliefs, to form a cohesive **community.**

Of the items recommended by the APA in their first code of ethics was respect for all people and their concomitant feelings, behaviors, and beliefs. It is often difficult to appreciate the feelings and beliefs of others when their beliefs are very different from our own.

1. Take a few moments and reflect on your values and beliefs. Pay particular attention to any strong or passionate beliefs that you may have. Then list as many of your values and beliefs as possible below.

2. Have you ever encountered someone with a different set of beliefs from your own?

3. Describe the situation and how you handled it.

# SOCIOLOGY

### *Let's All Hold Hands*

1. How can we as individuals exhibit the value of **community?**

2. As an online learner, to whom do we belong? how are we interdependent?

Reflection Activity

*The Global You*

*Directions*

1. Place a check next to the terms that most closely reflect your values on The Global You Handout.

2. Your instructor will provide the titles for each of the columns via the class discussion board. With which group did you most closely relate?

3. Post your reactions about the group with whom you have been identified. Include an explanation about whether or not you were surprised with the results.

4. Respond to two other students' reactions.

# THE GLOBAL YOU HANDOUT

| | | |
|---|---|---|
| Adherence | Affiliation/relationships | Adventure |
| Civic pride | Importance of heart and humanity in the workplace | Balance |
| Conformity | Calmness; unflappable under duress | Casualness toward authority |
| Conservatism | Fairness; civil rights | Diversity |
| Consistency and uniformity | Health and wellness | Fun |
| Dedication and sacrifice | Individualism | Informality |
| Delayed reward | Instant gratification | Nontraditional orientation toward time and space |
| Dependability | Involvement | Pragmatism |
| Discipline | Optimism | Self-reliance |
| Duty before pleasure | Participation and inclusion | Sense of family through friends |
| Hard work | Personal freedom | Global thinking |
| Honor | Personal gratification | Skepticism |
| Law and order | Personal growth | Technoliteracy |
| Preference for things on | Social justice a grand scale | |
| Logic | Stars of the show Center of attention | |
| Loyalty | Teamwork oriented | |
| Obedience | Youth | |
| Past oriented/history | | |
| Patience | | |
| Persistence | | |
| Respect for authority | | |
| Save and pay cash | | |

*Activity adapted from: Stringer, D., & Cassidy, P. A. (2003). 52 Activities for exploring values differences. Yarmouth, ME: Nicholas Brealey Publishing (p. 53–55).*

## Reach Out

1. Name the communities in which you are involved.

2. What are the characteristics of these communities?

3. What communities have you avoided?

4. What communities make you feel uncomfortable?

5. What are your reasons for the distance and the discomfort?

6. What ways can you reduce this separation or discomfort?

7. How can you apply the value of **community** in your interaction with other groups or communities?

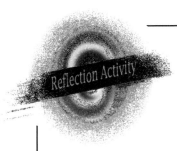

*Reflection Activity*

### Who Gets the Prized Jobs?

People can learn a lot about their ethnic or social class ranking and inequality in their society through a careful observation and evaluation of their own situation. The following activity is designed to help you do this.

1. Using the chart below, list 10 occupations.

2. Based on your own experience, write down the ethnicity, race, and gender of people in that occupation with whom you have had contact.

3. Rank the occupations in terms of status or prestige.

| Occupation | Ethnicity or Race | Gender |
| --- | --- | --- |
|  |  |  |
|  |  |  |
|  |  |  |
|  |  |  |
|  |  |  |
|  |  |  |
|  |  |  |
|  |  |  |
|  |  |  |
|  |  |  |

4. Next, tally the information for occupation, gender, and ethnicity or race.

5. What conclusions can you draw from the chart regarding ethnicity or race and gender?

6. Post your ranking and conclusions to the message board.

7. Respond to two other students' reactions.

*Adapted from: Stratification and Inequality, Enola K. Proctor, 1995.*

# CHAPTER 6

# RESPECT

*Look for your instructor's directions to complete the activities.*

*The word respect comes from the Latin word **Respectus,** meaning to "look back at." In the Rule, St. Benedict discusses respect where he refers to respecting others and respecting God. In our own time, we use the word respect to mean to have a regard for, or to look upon someone with great consideration or esteem, but the term has also come to include self-respect as an integral part of our own growth.*

## REFLECTION QUESTIONS

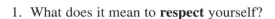

1. What does it mean to **respect** yourself?

2. Who is someone you **respect?** What is it about this person that makes you respect him or her?

3. How does **respect** influence your learning?

4. Do you show **respect** in the same way when viewing and responding to other students' comments on the class discussion board? Why or why not?

"Being brilliant is no great feat if you respect nothing."
—*Johann Wolfgang von Goethe*

"Surely, it is much easier to respect a man who has always had respect, than to respect a man who we know was last year no better than ourselves, and will be no better next year."
—*Samuel Johnson*

"No one is happy unless he respects himself."
—*Jean Jacques Rousseau*

### *Me, Myself, and My Reader*

When we think of the word "respect," we sometimes relegate it to interpersonal matters and face-to-face encounters. When we are children, we are taught to "respect our elders," to respect differences in others, and hopefully to respect ourselves. But what we don't often realize is that our writing is an extension of who we are, and by generating the wrong attitude or **tone** in our writing, we offer the impression to our readers that we have failed to respect them.

In both written and oral communication comes a great responsibility to communicate honestly, clearly, effectively, and with regard for your audience. The relationship between writers and their readers is very delicate. With a poor choice of words; a belittling tone; confused, overly long sentences; or unclear organization you can strain or jeopardize your relationship with your reader, severing communication. In addition, you can also appear to be uncaring, insincere, or disinterested in what you are saying so that you will fail to persuade your readers of your point of view. Essentially, careless writing creates an image of a careless person. And why should any reader attend to the words of someone who comes across as careless or thoughtless? It is often the case that people read what you write long before they see your face. In other words, you create an initial and very important first impression of yourself in your writing oftentimes BEFORE someone meets you. Whether you are writing a brief note or composing a memo, a cover letter, a job application, or a business report, you reveal who you are to your readers. They, in turn, create an initial impression of the person behind the written word. That is why it is essential that you reflect carefully on your writing—on the words you select, the sentences you construct, the examples or illustrations you provide.

**Tone** in writing refers to the writer's attitude toward his or her material. You communicate your tone in writing through your word choices, the style and length of your sentences, and even your punctuation.

The tone of a piece of writing can be formal or informal, humorous, impassioned, condescending, or angered; in short, it can take on any of the emotions you are feeling toward your subject at the time. Sometimes it may be appropriate to show anger or even sarcasm in a piece of writing if the subject and audience merits those attitudes. But it can be detrimental to your writing if the tone you select is inappropriate to your subject. Showing respect for the reader does not mean clouding your language with vague terms or euphemisms to distract, soften, or misrepresent your purpose, however. It does mean recognizing the power of language to build a relationship with your reader and effectively and convincingly communicate your point.

### Am I Funny? Am I Nice?

You can find a rich and varied array of voices and attitudes in newspaper and magazine articles. Below you'll find a few pieces of interesting reading from some very different magazines. Read through each excerpt and describe the tone of each piece. Then post your description on how tone affects both your enjoyment and your understanding of the writers' point of view toward their subjects on the class discussion board.

1. The following excerpt is taken from an article called "Viva Spanglish!" by Jonathon Keats. Keats discusses the rise of "Spanglish," a controversial mixture of English and Spanish that is on the rise in the United States.

   Spanglish doesn't belong to any particular region, yet there are realms in which even Aramaic would sound less foreign. . . . In business, speaking Spanglish is as good as declaring bankruptcy. And in society? Only disemboweling your host would be considered more gauche.

   Spanglish is a language of the impoverished—although by no means an impoverished language—a tongue that stigmatizes those who use it outside the barrio as if what they had to say were worthless. Yet, again like Yiddish in previous generations, it also links people thrown together from different countries and distant cities; it's an ad hoc umbilical cord among Americans newly born (46).

   Tone:_____

2. The next excerpt is from a book entitled *Dr. Fatkins' Resolutionary Diet*. A self-proclaimed "fantastic, fictitious diet for those who love cream cakes, chocolate, and buckets of fast food," the book is supposedly written by "Dr. I. B. Fatkins, Ph.D., M.B.A., F.A.T., M.S.N., T.U.B., C.S.E., MP3." The passage below contains Dr. Fatkins' commentary on diet myths.

   We've all been irritated by those career dieters who can reel off the caloric value, carbohydrate content, and percentage of saturated fat level in every single element of your meal. Don't you wish you could knock their smug smile off their perfectly proportioned size-four body? Well, now you can as Dr. Fatkins reveals the myths behind these figures.

   For a start, carrots . . . how many calories in a common carrot? Ten? Thirty? One hundred? Would you believe me if I said 976? It is true; one carrot has the same amount of calories a bag of tortilla chips has (unless it's BBQ flavor, which actually has a negative calorific effect). Mistakes made in the original calculation of dietary values have never been corrected and years of repetition have created the myth. Other frighteningly fattening foods include scallions, celery, chicken breast (white only), and bottled water (some of which is also illegally calorie-enhanced). (34)

   Tone:_____

3. The third excerpt is taken from the April 5, 2004 issue of *The New Yorker*. The article is "The Height Gap" by Birkhard Bilger.

Over the past thirty years, a new breed of "anthropometric historians" has tracked how populations around the world have changed in stature. Height, they've concluded, is a kind of biological shorthand: a composite code for all the factors that make up a society's well-being. Height variations within a population are largely genetic, but height variations between populations are mostly environmental, anthropometric history suggests. If Joe is taller than Jack, it's probably because his parents are taller. But if the average Norwegian is taller than the average Nigerian it's because Norwegians live healthier lives. That's why the United Nations now uses height to monitor nutrition in developing countries. In our height lies the tale of our birth and upbringing, of our social class, daily diet, and health-care coverage. In our height lies our history (38–39).

Tone:_____

Question: How does tone affect both your enjoyment and your understanding of the writers' point of view toward their subjects?

### No Jeers for Your Peers

Often you will be asked to adopt the role of a peer editor for a classmate's work. Peer editing is a very common exercise, especially in your composition classes. But it is also an exercise that can be easily misunderstood or mishandled. If done irresponsibly, the role of a peer editor can erode into the role of a flattering, excessively polite admirer ("I love your essay. It's the best thing I've ever read. I wouldn't change a thing! A++++"); an insulting, pejorative critic ("Man! An 8-year-old could have written something better than this!"); or a vague, general reader ("The intro was OK. . . . You used examples. . . . I liked the ending. . . . Sometimes sentences were hard to understand. . . ."). Any of these poses leaves the writer without specific, useful information. Your role as a peer editor is to critique a writer's work by offering helpful, objective pointers. Don't hesitate telling a writer about the particularly effective parts of his or her work; positive comments are useful and encouraging. Just make sure to balance the compliments with commentary that will strengthen the writer's work. The process requires respect for the writer. It's not always an easy task to lay open your work for someone else to critique. It is often one of the most helpful ways, however, to gain some perspective on your work.

Beyond the guidelines your instructor will offer for peer editing, keep the following points in mind when you are editing someone's paper:

1. Choose an appropriate **tone.** Unless you intimately know the writer, avoid joking about the work: your intentions could easily be misinterpreted. Keep to an interested, concerned voice of an impartial observer.

2. Decide on the level of formality of your word choices based upon your relationship to the writer. For example, an informal tone that uses a specialized slang or jargon won't be of much use to a reader who does not share your specialized language.

3. Be specific. General or unexplained statements like "great," "weak," "I like it," or "I didn't understand" will be of no use to a writer unless you follow-up with some particulars or examples.

4. Don't be insulting. No matter how bad you think a work is, insulting the writer only damages his or her confidence. You have a responsibility to honestly critique the work, not to bash it. Balance any negative comment by explaining the problem in detail to the writer and offering suggestions for improvement.

### Directions

1. Select an editorial from a reputable online news source that you think is particularly poorly written.

2. E-mail the editorial to a classmate your instructor has chosen.

3. Edit the piece you received from your classmate keeping in mind the four points above.

4. Return your critique to your classmate.

5. Read each other's critiques.

6. How successful was your classmate in being honest yet respectful toward the writer? E-mail your points to your classmate.

### *The Chairman, the Businessman, and the Stewardess*

Respecting your reader also means choosing words carefully to avoid offending, stereotyping, or denigrating the reader. Using a term like "chairman" or "businessman" for example, assumes that only men can hold those positions. Of primary concern in writing today is avoiding **sexist language.** Sexist language is using gender-specific words that may exclude a group. Words like chair**man,** spokes**man,** stewardess, or fire**man** presume that only one gender can hold these roles. Be sensitive to supplying alternatives for these kinds of words: chairman can easily be converted to chair**person,** spokesman to spokes**person,** stewardess to flight attendant, and fireman to firefighter.

In English, avoiding sexist language is also complicated because we have no singular, neutral pronoun. For example, read the following sentence:

> A writer has his own writing style.

In order to achieve correct agreement between the pronoun (his) and its antecedent (the word the pronoun refers to, in this case "writer"), you'll have to use a singular pronoun, which will create sexist language. It used to be common to use the masculine singular pronoun in sentences requiring a singular pronoun. Now, however, that is no longer a generally accepted convention. In communication, try to replace sexist language with **gender-inclusive or gender-neutral** language. Here are a few easy options to ensure you are respecting your reader: (1) include BOTH the singular masculine and feminine pronoun as in "his or her" or "his/her" as in:

> A writer has his or her own writing style.

or (2) change the noun to a plural and use a plural pronoun:

> Writers have their own writing styles.

Rewriting the sentence and trading off the singular for the plural often takes care of the problem of sexist language without having to depend upon the more wordy "his or her" option. Unless you are certain of the gender of your readers, you will have to make a choice for your writing in order to avoid sexist language.

### *Directions*

Now that you are more acquainted with sexist language and the effect it may have on your readers, re-read the quotations that open this chapter on respect. Do you find any that use what we would today consider to be sexist language? Rephrase these quotations to remove sexist language and post your rewrites on the class discussion board.

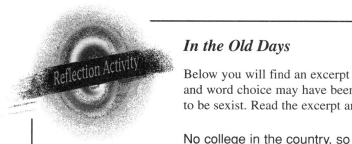

Reflection Activity

### In the Old Days

Below you will find an excerpt from an 1887 issue of *Scribner's Magazine*. Although the tone and word choice may have been acceptable to readers of the day, today we might find the article to be sexist. Read the excerpt and then complete the questions that follow.

No college in the country, so far as I know, gives instruction on all matters included in the study of English in its widest sense. None provides the requisite facilities for a student who desires to master his mother tongue in its history as a language, in its completeness as a literature, and in its full scope as a means of expression with the pen and with the lips. This state of things is not, and has not been for many years, the case with Greek, Latin, or mathematics. It is no longer the case with many branches of natural science, with some of the modern languages, or with some of the most ancient ones. Why should it be so with English? Why should a man who wishes to know all that is to be known about the language he is going to use all his life be at a disadvantage in the pursuit of his favorite species of knowledge, as compared with him whose tastes lead him to regions into which only a few specialists are privileged to enter?

The question answers itself. There is every reason why every college in the country should do for English all that it does for its most favored studies; and the time will come, or I greatly misread the signs of the future, when no American institution of learning can afford to economize in this direction. Now that learned men and learned bodies are, like clergy-men and churches, no longer too far above the rest of the world to be weighed in the same scales in which other men and other bodies are weighed, and to be criticized with equal freedom, they can no longer apply the resources supplied by public or by private beneficence to the nourishment of hobby-horses whose bones are marrow-less, in whose eyes there is either no speculation in the old sense of that word, or too much speculation in the modern sense. A college, which is to live by the people, must supply the education needed for the people, and for the leaders of the people; and what is so much needed as English? In these days of multifarious knowledge, of intellectual activity in so many directions, there are many things of which a man need know only the rudiments: but of English an educated man should know more than the rudiments, because if for no other reason everybody knows, or half-knows, or thinks he knows them; because everybody deems himself capable, not only of criticizing the English of others, but also of writing good English himself. Therefore, educated men should know enough to be able to protect pure English against the numerous foes that beset it on every side in these days of free speech and a free press.

### Questions

1. What is the writer's attitude toward studying English in college?

2. What assumptions does the writer make about the audience?

3. How might the article be guilty of using sexist language by today's standards?

4. After reading and posting your responses to questions 1-3 on the discussion board, rewrite the article, updating it to more modern language. Remove all sexist language and replace it with non-sexist language that might be more acceptable to today's reader.

Reflection Activity

### *Tell Me a Story*

Literature affords us many opportunities to reflect upon ourselves, our views of others, and our biases, beliefs, and values. Read the poem "Sure You Can Ask Me a Personal Question" by Diane Burns and answer the discussion questions. This poem can be found in its entirety through a search at
http://cc.ysu.edu/~asleskov/sure%2C_you_can_ask_me.htm

1. What are three different kinds of stereotypes found in the poem?

2. How would you describe the speaker's tone?

3. What are the effects of stereotyping on the speaker of the poem?

4. How would you describe the person the speaker is addressing?

5. What value or values are being disregarded by the person the speaker is addressing?

*Reflection Activity*

## Your Turn

1.  Identify another group that is stereotyped in society (women, the disabled, minorities, etc.). Then write a poem similar to "Sure You Can Ask Me a Personal Question," which illustrates how one stereotypes a particular group.

2.  Post your poem on the class discussion board. Share your experiences in writing the poem. What surprised you? What did you like or dislike about the experience of writing the poem?

# MATHEMATICS

*Reflection Activity*

### Anticipation Guide

### Directions

1. Read each statement in the box below. Under the **Before Reading** column, write *Yes* if you feel you could support the statement. If you feel you could not support the statement then write *No*.

| Before Reading | Statements | After Reading |
|---|---|---|
| | Women find it difficult to succeed in the field of mathematics. | |
| | In the early 1900s it was best that most universities did not admit women. | |
| | People from different cultures may experience adversity in pursuing certain academic subjects. | |
| | Women excel at subjects like art, literature, and music. | |
| | People cannot usually combat the prejudices of their time. | |

2. Read the article about Emmy Noether.

## On a Tangent

Emmy Noether: Premier Woman Mathematician

One of the people to establish significant results in the area of abstract algebra was Emmy Noether (1882–1935). She was perhaps the most creative woman mathematician of all time. She succeeded in her mathematics research in the face of two cultural factors of her time that made success—in fact, existence—difficult: She was female and she was Jewish.

She grew up in the town of Erlangen in southern Germany and graduated from a girls' high school. Three years later, in 1900, she passed a test to qualify as a teacher of French and English. About this time she became interested in mathematics and in pursuing university studies. In 1900 she was one of two women allowed to audit, but not take for credit, classes at the University of Erlangen. In 1904 the University of Erlangen permitted women to register and she became a regular student. In 1908 she received her doctorate, specializing in abstract algebra.

She lived with her family in Erlangen for seven years until in 1915 David Hilbert, the most influential mathematician of the time, invited her to the University of Göttingen (Germany), the leading university in mathematics at that time. Although as a woman she was not allowed to teach courses or to receive a salary, Hilbert arranged for her to teach courses given under his name. Hilbert also spoke to the university senate in favor of appointing her to a position of *Privatdozent:* "I do not see that the sex of the candidate is an argument against her admission as *Privatdozent*. After all, the Senate is not a bathhouse." Hilbert had much more influence in the mathematical community than he had on Noether's appointment. It was not until changes in Germany after World War I that she finally became a *Privatdozent* at Göttingen in 1919.

Noether continued to teach at Göttingen until 1933, when the Nazis were in power and attacking both Jews and nonconforming mathematicians. In that year the university dismissed her. The Nazi machine effectively dismantled the premier mathematical institution in the world of the time and caused the locus of mathematical activity to be redistributed around the world. Noether accepted a visiting professorship at Bryn Mawr College in Pennsylvania. She died suddenly in 1935, after only about two years in the United States.

Her work through the years in abstract algebra established her as one of the significant mathematicians of the twentieth century and as probably the principal woman mathematician of all time.

*Source: Beers, K. (2003).* When kids can't read: What teachers can do. *Portsmouth, NH: Heinemann.*

3. Reread the statements in the box above. Now respond to each statement again as to whether you could or could not support them and write *Yes* or *No* in the **After Reading** column.

4. Share your thoughts about one of the statements on the class discussion board.

5. How would you connect this article and the information found in it to the core value of **respect**?

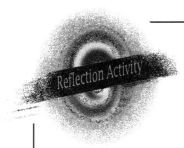

### Bills, Bills, Bills

| | |
|---|---|
| **OBJECTIVES:** | To provide practical, hands-on experience in solving interrelated linear equations as an introduction to simultaneous equations. |
| | To provide an opportunity to design a professional presentation and spreadsheet. |
| | To demonstrate respect in a team approach activity. (Instructor will place students in teams.) |
| **SOURCE:** | The McClure Company, St. Petersburg, Florida |
| **BACKGROUND:** | You will act as a shopping center leasing team responsible for tenant billing. You will be expected to use exploration and experimentation to determine an efficient and accurate method for breaking down bills that are sent to the shopping center. Your team must interpret meter-reading results and determine how to best divide the bill according to retail space, energy use, and meter readings. |
| **THE PROBLEM:** | A shopping center is billed as a single entity and the management team must divide, distribute, and collect bills from each tenant. This is a timely process and a spreadsheet can be used to simplify the process in future months. The process must be legal, defendable, and must accurately cover all costs. You are provided with the billing statement from Bellair Plaza in Daytona Beach, Florida, along with retail space, tenant descriptions, and two monthly water-reading totals. Your team must use the data to design a spreadsheet model that can be used to automatically break down and print the tenants' bills in future months by updating the meter readings and total bill. You will need to design individual bills while ensuring that the total amount billed out covers the total amount due. Each bill can be modeled with a linear equation simultaneously satisfying the master bill. |

### BELLAIR PLAZA
North Atlantic Avenue
Daytona Beach, Florida

## Tenants:

### Publix

Occupies 25,600 sq. ft. and has continued occupancy through 06/31/05 at the present rate of $1.25 per square foot (psf) and percentage rent of sales over $3,199,992 at a rate of 1%. Current sales are over the percentage rent breakpoint.

## Winn-Dixie

Winn-Dixie occupies 21,877 sq. ft. and has continued occupancy through 4/30/02 at the current rate of $4.84 psf. Percentage rent is applicable at a rate of 1% on sales over $9,535,000. Winn-Dixie would like to expand this store.

## Walgreen Drugs

Walgreen's occupies 11,970 sq. ft. and has occupancy through 3/31/06. The present rate of rent is $10.00 psf with increases of $0.50 scheduled for 4/1/05 and 4/1/10. Percentage rent is applicable at a rate of 2% on sales over $7,007,298.

## Blockbuster

Blockbuster occupies 6,400 sq. ft. and the present rate of rent is $13.00 psf. The lease runs through 6/31/06 and they have two and five-year renewal options with established rates on years 1–2 at $12.00 psf and years 3–4 at $13.00 psf. The remainder of the renewal option for the rent is to be negotiated.

## TCBY Yogurt

Currently occupying 1,375 sq. ft. with a rent based at $14.50 psf.

## Salty Dog Surf and Apparel

Pays $21.00 psf on 3,425 sq. ft. for an annual rent of $71,925.

## Pizza Hut Delivery

Current rent is $18,700 annually for 1,100 sq. ft.

## Best Realty

Leases 1,100 sq. ft. at a rate of $19.00 psf.

## Subway

Pays $18.00 psf for 1,100 sq. ft. of space.

## SuperCuts

Lease is for 825 sq. ft. with a rent of $19.47 psf.

The summer office support, must design an accounting form to produce a monthly bill for the seven tenants in one branch of the center, including charges for water, sewage, and garbage.

### *Billing Criteria*

The water and sewage bill should be broken down according to actual water used; see meter readings.

- The garbage bill should be broken down as follows:

  —The food establishments should split half of the bill with TCBY paying a set rate of $125.00 per month.

  —The remaining establishments should split the other half of the bill according to square footage occupied.

- The storm water will be broken down as follows:

  —Blockbuster will pay $5.02, Salty Dog Surf and Apparel will pay $7.53, and all other tenants will pay a set rate of $2.51.

---

**Water Meter Readings**

City of Daytona Beach Utility Bill

| | |
|---|---|
| • Customer Name: | Bellair Plaza |
| • Garbage and yard dump: | $ 594.42 |
| • Water: | $ 149.85 |
| • Sewer: | $ 251.95 |
| • Storm Water: | $ 20.48 |
| • Recycling: | $ 285.00 |
| Total bill: | $1,301.70 |

---

## Your Assignment

Design a spreadsheet using Microsoft Excel that can be used as a bill to be sent to the tenant each month. The bill should contain a total charge, previous and current meter readings, and a break down of the bill including water, sewer, garbage, recycling, and storm water. You should have an individual bill for each of the tenants listed on the meter reading, along with a summary for the property owners. **Respect** should be implied, defined, and clearly stated as a general guideline in completing this assignment with your team.

## Project Requirements

- A summary statement listing all tenant charges and the total bill.
- A bill for each of the following tenants:

| | |
|---|---|
| Best Realty | Subway |
| Blockbuster | SuperCuts |
| Pizza Hut | TCBY |
| Salty Dog | |

1. Did every team member actively participate?

2. Did anyone dominate in your team?

3. Did all team members **respect** each role equally?

4. How did each member contribute to the overall project?

5. Did you observe mutual **respect** among team members? Why or why not?

6. Do you strongly feel that **respect** for everyone's ideas is necessary in working as a team? Why or why not?

# HISTORY

**Reflection Activity**

## *Children at Work*

The age of industrialism took its toll on its workers, who often worked six days a week, ten hours a day. But not just the adults worked in the factories. "By 1900, the industrial labor force included some 1.7 million children" (Davidson, et al., p. 481). In addition to long hours, workers were also forced to work in unsafe environments. In fact, close to 700 people were killed on the job weekly. These children, such as the ones pictured below illustrate the conditions of the time for these young workers.

Examine each photograph closely, and then answer the following questions:

*Sadie, a cotton mill spinner, Lancaster, South Carolina, 1908*

*Mill Boy from The National Archives*

From Library of Congress, Prints and Photographs Division, FSA/OWI Collection.

1. How old do you think the Mill Boy is?

2. What is a mill?

3. Describe his surroundings. Are they safe? Why or why not?

4. Why do you think he is not in school?

5. How old do you think Sadie is?

6. In the image of Sadie, what dominates the image, to what are your eyes drawn?

7. How do these photographs give you insight into industrialization?

8. What kind of effects did industrialization have on families?

9. Do you feel that their employers respected these young workers? by their parents? Why or why not?

*Reflection Activity*

### Slave Song

Read the slave song below and then answer the questions that follow.

See these poor souls from Africa

Transported to America.

We are stolen, and sold in Georgia,

Will you go along with me?

We are stolen, and sold in Georgia,

Come sound the jubilee!

See wives and husbands sold apart,

Their children's screams will break my heart—

There's a better day a coming,

Will you go along with me?

There's a better day a coming,

Go sound the jubilee!

O, gracious Lord! When shall it be,

That we poor souls shall all be free,

Lord, break them slavery powers,

Will you go along with me?

Lord break them slavery powers,

Go sound the jubilee!

Dear Lord, dear Lord, when slavery'll cease,

Then we poor souls will have our peace.

There's a better day a coming,

Will you go along with me?

There's a better day a coming,

Go sound the jubilee!

*Source: This poem is recorded by William Wells Brown in his book,* Narrative of an American Slave *(1849), p. 51.*

1. Name some examples of the unfair treatment that the slaves sang about in this song.

2. Relate your examples of the unfair treatment of slaves from question one, to the core value of **respect**. Did we, as Americans at the time, respect the slaves? Give support for your answer.

3. Do you detect any amount of hope from this slave song? Give support for your answer.

*Reflection Activity*

*World News*

Read an article of international consequence in the newspaper, magazine, or online.

Answer the following questions:

1.  Summarize the article in the box below.

| Title of Article: | **WORLD NEWS** |
|---|---|
|  |  |

2.  How does this event affect you? your family? your peers?

3.  Predict what it would be like if this event occurred at your university.

4.  Which value would be most significant in dealing with the topic?

5.  Now, imagine that **respect** was omitted from or added to this event. What would the situation look like then?

# PSYCHOLOGY

## The Three R's

The **respect** that a therapist demonstrates for a client's feelings is very similar to the core value of **respect.** We are encouraged to listen to those in our academic community and demonstrate appreciation for thoughts, ideas, or emotions that are different than our own. Although this sounds relatively easy, it is certainly no small task. Consider how many times you have discounted or dismissed something that a friend, family member, or classmate has told you. Indeed, demonstrating **respect** for others is a characteristic that all students and faculty alike must strive to demonstrate when interacting with those around us.

Among the tools that psychologists use in therapy, few are as powerful as the use of *affect.* Affect can be broadly defined as a feeling or emotion, but can be more specifically described as an emotional response to a person, situation, or event. During the course of therapeutic interaction, patients will frequently display various affective changes and may indicate that they are experiencing feelings either based on something that has happened, is happening, or that they perceive will happen. When working with these patients, it is very important to focus on **R**espectful, **R**eflective, and **R**esponding in an effort to effect patient change.

### Event/Affect Chart

### Directions

In the first column, describe a dramatic event that happened at some point in your life. In the affect column, describe how you responded to the event.

| Event | Affect |
|-------|--------|
|       |        |
|       |        |
|       |        |
|       |        |

**Final thought**: The various words that you use to describe your feelings will likely change depending on your mood, the day of the week, or the events that have recently transpired in your life. Regardless of what feelings are expressed by someone else, it is important that as therapists we (a) identify the feeling experienced either in the words used by the individual or in our own words, (b) acknowledge that the individual is experiencing the feelings and offer support, and (c) respect the feelings provided and make an effort to convey the respect in our demeanor towards others.

## *Personal Culture*

## *Directions*

Read the passage below.

One of the areas in which many people may feel disrespected by others involves culture. Culture can largely be defined as the amalgamation of our personal values and beliefs, experience in the world, racial, ethnic, and socioeconomic background. Ramsey (1996, p. 9), likened culture to an abstraction; it cannot actually be seen or touched. The analogy of the wind is helpful in grasping the abstract and secondhand nature of this concept. One cannot see the wind. So how do we know it is a windy day? We see a flag moving, we hear leaves of a tree rubbing against each other, and we feel pressure on our skin. The name we give the difference or the feeling is "wind." So too with culture. We see people acting in agreed-upon ways in the face of similar situations . . . and, we say, "Oh, those people belong to the same culture."

Certainly, culture is a critical element to who we are. However, individuals often do not recognize the importance of our cultural background, and people frequently disrespect our personal origins. As a matter of fact, although many theorists, writers, and researchers within the field of psychology have recognized the need for special considerations in therapy when working with racial or ethnic minority groups, the profession of psychology has demonstrated little concerted effort in confronting many important issues related to minority concerns until only very recently. The American Psychological Association (APA) first recommended that therapists and practitioners attain specific competency to work with racially and culturally diverse clients in 1973, and prior to that, many theoretical writings described treatment with diverse clients as the facilitation, instillation, and development of mainstream values and beliefs in those individuals with cultural backgrounds different from the majority view (Pope–Davis, Menefee, & Ottavi, 1993).

Since these early understandings of working with diverse groups, however, revised editions of the APA's Code of Ethics have included as a provision, sensitivity to, and respect for racially and culturally diverse populations. Further, the APA released a document in 1993, which specified guidelines applicable to all service providers working with diverse groups. An important proviso contained in this document implied that to act in an ethically consistent manner, psychologists were required to attain a minimum level of proficiency in treating racial or ethnic minority clients through the acquisition and exhibition of multicultural counseling competencies.

The APA has continued to espouse awareness that individuals emanate from unique cultural experiences and thus should not all be treated identically. In psychology, it is considered unethical behavior to ignore diversity issues when working with clients. So, too, in the university environment, the Saint Leo University core values of **respect** and **community** encourage us to treat everyone fairly and judiciously, and to forge deep affiliation bonds with one another regardless of differences we may perceive in color, race, ethnicity, socioeconomic status, gender, age, sexual orientation, or religious

From Siobhan Herkert

predilection. As indicated by Saint Benedict himself, there can be no university without community and global appreciation that each member of the community contributes something very useful to the whole. As such, we as students and faculty of Saint Leo University are challenged to work in concert with one another to develop relational bonds and a deepened appreciation of one another in an effort to aspire to the core values of **respect** and **community** as conceptualized under the Rule of Saint Benedict.

Complete the Four-Column Journal by doing the following:

1. Summarize the passage "Personal Culture" in the first column.

2. Write a personal response to the passage in the second column.

3. Post your response to the class discussion board.

4. Respond to another classmate's response.

5. Read what your classmates wrote about your response, and write these comments in the third column.

6. Write a final reflection in the last column.

## FOUR-COLUMN JOURNAL

| Summary | My Response | Peer Response | My Response |
|---------|-------------|---------------|-------------|
|         |             |               |             |

*Source: Hill, B. C., Noe, K. S., & King, J. A. (2003).* Literature Circles in Middle School: One Teacher's Journey. *Norwood, MA. Christopher-Gordon Publishing, Inc.*

Reflection Activity

### Three-Column Notes

Compare and contrast the six core values with the Ethical Principles of Psychologists and Code of Conduct (2002) by the American Psychological Association (APA). First, review the definitions of the six core values: excellence, community, respect, personal development, responsible stewardship, and integrity. Then, go to the Appendix to review the Ethical Principles of Psychologists and Code of Conduct (2002) which can also be found at the following website: http://www2.apa.org/ethics/code2002.doc

### Directions

1. In the left-hand column write those characteristics that are particular to the six core values.
2. In the right-hand column write those characteristics that are particular to the APA's Ethical Principles.
3. In the center column write the characteristics that are common to both.

| Characteristics of Core Values | Characteristics of Both | Characteristics of Ethical Principles |
|---|---|---|
| | | |

# SOCIOLOGY

## *We Are All in This Together*

Have you asked yourself why people act, think, and believe the way they do? Well, the social sciences disciplines seek to answer questions like these and more about individuals, groups, and societies. The disciplines that make up the social sciences include sociology, psychology, anthropology, economics, geography, history, and political science. Each discipline asks different questions about human behavior and the social environment. For example, psychology focuses on individuals and what factors shape a person's personality, mind, and behavior. Sociology focuses on groups and how relationships are formed within groups and how groups interact with each other.

Every human group consists of *culture,* which is the group's language, beliefs, values, norms, and material objects that are passed from generation to generation. Have you ever wondered why a friend's family had different beliefs from your family? Did you ever think they were odd or strange? A common characteristic of all groups is called ethnocentrism—where a group believes its way of life is the best. You use your culture as the standard by which all other groups are judged. However, as you have interacted with different groups, perhaps, you have found their different values interesting. Hopefully you tried to understand their values or way of life from their point of view rather than judging from only your view of life.

Some of the topics sociology studies are groups' treatment of other people based on race, gender, social class, values; how groups decide who is a part of the in-group and who is part of the out-group; and why some groups get most of the power, prestige, and wealth, while others do not.

Values are an essential aspect of culture and therefore an integral part of the study of sociology. How do values influence thoughts, actions, and beliefs of people and society? In other words, how do your values shape the way you are as a person and how you interact with your social world? Let's get into this topic by completing assignments on the value of respect:

1. As individuals how can we **respect** unique talents, ensure dignity, foster unity, promote diversity, and the free exchange of ideas?

2. How can the university's administration, faculty, and staff **respect** unique talents, ensure dignity, foster unity, promote diversity, and the free exchange of idea?

3. Post your responses to questions 1 and 2 to the class discussion board.

"Let's get one thing straight. I don't want your money, I want your respect."

From www.CartoonStock.com

### *Geeks, Nerds, and Dumb Blondes*

People often are unaware of how they are socialized to view and treat groups differently than their own. The following exercise will raise awareness of how stereotypes influence how individuals respect or fail to respect other groups.

1. What individuals or groups have you referred to by stereotypes or name-calling?

2. Have you met all individuals from groups with whom you have stereotyped?

3. How and from what source(s) did you learn about these stereotypes?

4. How do you define who is in your "in-group" and who is in your "out-group"?

5. With which group do you identify? Describe your experiences being in this group.

*Reflection Activity*

## *Who's In and Who's Out?*

**social group**  A group of people who share a range of physical, cultural, or social characteristics within one of the categories of social identity.

### SOCIAL GROUP MEMBERSHIPS

| | |
|---|---|
| Gender: | Female, male, transgender people |
| Race: | Black, White, Latino, Asian or Pacific Islander, Native American, Biracial |
| Ethnicity: | African-American, Cuban, English, Chinese, Sioux |
| Sexual Orientation: | Bisexual, lesbian, Gay, homosexual |
| Religion: | Christian, Jew, Muslim, Hindu |
| Class: | Poor, working class, middle class, owning class |
| Age: | Young people, young adults, middle-aged adults, elderly |

### SOCIAL GROUP MEMBERSHIP PROFILE

| Social Identities | Membership | Status |
|---|---|---|
| Gender<br>Race<br>Ethnicity<br>Sexual Orientation<br>Religion<br>Class<br>Age | | |

1. In the membership column on the preceding page, identify and write *your* social group membership for each social identity category (i.e., race, gender, class).

2. Which of your social group memberships were easiest to identify?

3. Which of your social group memberships were most difficult to identify?

*Source: Adams, M., Bell, L. A., & Griffin, P., pp. 70–74.*

## Differences in Commonalities

| RACE | Whites | Blacks, Latinos, Asians, Native Americans, biracial people |
|---|---|---|
| CLASS | Men | Women |
| SEXUAL ORIENTATION | Heterosexual | Lesbians, gay men, bisexual people |
| RELIGION | Gentiles, Christians | Jews, Muslims, Hindus |
| ABILITY | Nondisabled people | Disabled people |
| AGE | Young and middle-aged adults | Young people, old people |

Refer to the Differences in Commonalities table above and answer the following questions:

1. What do you notice about how different social groups are arranged in the second column and in the third column?

2. What do the social groups in each column have in common?

   **Note:** What you have just identified are differences in status between groups.

3. Go back to the social group membership profile textbox and identify your status (i.e., advantaged or disadvantaged) for each of your social group memberships. (i.e., Native Americans—disadvantaged)

4. For which social group memberships was it easiest to identify your status?

5. For which social group memberships was it more difficult to identify your status?

6. When you look at your overall profile, what surprises you?

7. Which social group members are you most aware of on a daily basis?

8. Which ones are you least aware of?

9. Which ones would you like to learn more about?

10. How does this social membership profile activity relate to the core value of **respect?**

*Source: Adams, M., Bell, L. A., & Griffin, P., pp. 70–74.*

*Reflection Activity*

### *The People Next Door . . .*

Complete each statement. There is no right or wrong answer.

1. I have lived among people of: (check all that apply)

   _____ other cultures      _____ other classes      _____ other ethnic backgrounds

_____ other religious backgrounds      _____ other races      _____ other sexual orientation

How many check marks do you have? _____

2. One value of the culture that I grew up in is:


3. One thing my parents or family taught me about my

   Gender: _____

   Ethnicity: _____

   Race: _____


4. One thing my parents or family taught me about

   Gay and lesbian people: _____

   Jewish people: _____

   White people: _____


5. My biggest concern about meeting and working with people who are different from me is:


*Source: Enola K. Proctor's book, Race, Gender, and Class: Guidelines for Practice with Individuals, 1995.*

### *Resolving Conflicts*

1. Read the following quote.

When we have conflicts in values, they are rarely identified as such. If two people differ in appearance (color, gender, ethnicity, disability, etc.), the conflict is often attributed to that difference. If there is no visible difference, the conflict is usually attributed to 'personality differences.' It is much easier to resolve conflicts when the source of the conflict has been accurately identified (Stringer & Cassiday, 171).

2. Reflecting on past conflicts that you have encountered in your life and the passage from above, write a short response below as to how you would characterize these past disagreements.

3. The core value of **respect** states that we should be open to a free exchange of ideas. Keeping this in mind, how do you see yourself handling conflicts in the future?

"I called this emergency meeting to discuss the lack of respect I've been getting around here lately."

From www.CartoonStock.com

## Evolutionism vs Creationism

The core value of **respect** states that a community's strength depends on the free exchange of ideas and learning. Given that, and your course readings on Darwin's theory of evolution, as well as your own personal views, complete the graphic organizer below.

### Directions

1. Read the statement below.
   *There is no place for evolution in a culture that believes in creation.*

2. List information or arguments on the "yes" side that would support the statement.

3. List information or arguments on the opposite side that would support a "no" answer.

4. Which side is more compelling?

5. Post your "compelling side" on the class discussion board.

6. Respond to another classmate's response.

| YES | NO |
|-----|-----|
|     |     |

*Source: Irvin, J. L., Buehl, D. R., & Klemp, R. M. (2003).* Reading and the high school student: Strategies to enhance literacy. *Boston: Allyn and Bacon.*

### *The Struggles of Galileo and Darwin*

Galileo struggled most of his life to have his ideas about science accepted. At the time (late 1500s–1600s) the scientific writings of Aristotle were accepted as absolute truth. Yet, Galileo found many errors with Aristotle's scientific views, which made him very unpopular and prompted him to leave Pisa, Italy. Galileo also supported the Copernican system, which was opposed by the church. Because of Galileo's scientific beliefs, he was briefly imprisoned in Rome and forced to deny his belief. Although he was confined to his home during the latter years of his life by order of the church and forced not to write about astronomy again, he continued to live a productive life, providing the groundwork for modern physics.

Just like Galileo, so too did Charles Darwin struggle with his own scientific views. After coming to the conclusion that all species of plants and animals evolved over time through natural selection, Darwin was afraid to publish his findings for fear of punishment. Instead he married and settled down in southern England. During this time his health suffered greatly making him a semi-invalid, due in part to a disease from an insect bite from his voyages, and from the strain of keeping his view of evolution a secret. Finally, after 20 years Darwin published his book, *On the Origin of Species* knowing it would likely ruin his reputation as a respected scholar, cause pain to his wife, a devout Christian, and threaten his children's future. It immediately created uproar and he was ridiculed and maligned greatly. However, after only a few years, Darwin's theory became accepted by much of the scientific community. Interestingly enough, his health improved greatly with his theory's acceptance.

1. If you knew your research would be perceived as a threat towards society and might endanger your own life, would you uphold the norm or continue to pursue your radical ideas?

2. Relate the struggles of Galileo and Darwin to the core value of **respect.**

# CHAPTER 7

# PERSONAL DEVELOPMENT

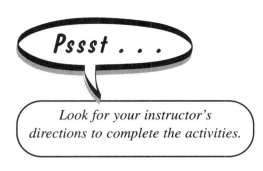

*Pssst . . .*

Look for your instructor's
directions to complete the activities.

*Personal Development is only complete when the whole person—mind, body, and spirit—function in total harmony. And it is the human spirit, the inner person that radiates faith, virtue, and values to the outer person. As Proverbs puts it, "The spirit of man is the candle of the Lord, searching all the inner depths of his heart" (20:27).*

### REFLECTION QUESTIONS

1. Do you think the development of the body is connected to the development of the mind?

2. How do you balance the development of mind, body, and spirit?

3. Does our culture emphasize one aspect of **personal development** over another?

"Behold the turtle. He only makes progress when he sticks his neck out."
—*James Bryant Conant*

"I do the best I know how, the very best I can; and I mean to keep on doing it until the end. If the end brings me out all right, what is said against me will not amount to anything. If the end brings me out all wrong, ten angels swearing I was right would make no difference."
—*Abraham Lincoln*

"Keep away from people who try to belittle your ambitions. Small people do that, but the really great make you feel that you, too, can somehow become great."
—*Mark Twain*

"Ok, now what?"

# FINE ARTS

### *Canvas, Concrete, or Clay*

1. Read a biography of one of the following artists: Michelangelo, Leonardo da Vinci, Mozart, Picasso, or Frank Lloyd Wright.

2. How is their artwork evidence of their journey toward **personal development?**

*Reflection Activity*

### Seek and Ye Shall Find

1. A lot of artwork tends to depict the spiritual quest of the artist. Log onto one of the following virtual museums to discover a painting or sculpture whose images you think depict this quest.

### Virtual Museum Websites:
http://www.amn.org
http://www.fno.org/museum/muse.html
http://www.diegorivera.com
http://www.wetcanvas.com/Museum/
http://icom.museum/vlmp/
http://www.virtualfreesites.com/museums.html

2. Write a brief response describing the spiritual quest of the artist.

3. Draw or otherwise create a visual representation of your quest for **personal development.**

# PERSONAL WELLNESS

1. Describe your overall physical fitness. On a scale of 1–5, with 1 being poor physical condition, and 5 excellent physical condition, where would you put yourself?

2. Do you exercise? If so, how often? If not, what is holding you back from exercising?

3. In reviewing the quotes in the text boxes throughout the chapter, choose one that best fits your lifestyle. Explain why you chose this quote.

"To master yourself, you must first master your habits; otherwise they will quickly master you."

—*Father Francis J. Peffley*

"Start the day by looking yourself in the eye and making the commitment to do and be your best that day."

—*Father Francis J. Peffley*

*Smoke-Free Pubs*

*Directions*

    1. Read the article *Today is the last day you can puff away in an Irish pub.*

## THE WORLD
## Today is the last day you can puff away in an Irish pub

*Associated Press*

DUBLIN, Ireland—Ireland is about to ban tobacco from workplaces, but rebellion hangs heavy in the air—particularly in that smokiest of places, the pub.

"I won't be enforcing it and I won't be telling my staff to enforce it, simple as that," pub owner Danny Healy-Rae said of the ban, which takes effect Monday and applies to any enclosed work space—more than 10,000 pubs, as well as billiard halls, private clubs, home offices, even a lone trucker's cab.

"We've a busy enough job to do here as it is, and we can't be chasing people into the television lounge or the toilets," added Healy-Rae, whose pub is in the County Kerry village of Kilgarvan—where, as is typical in rural Ireland, most customers smoke.

"We'll have to just let everyone smoke away as usual and the hell with what they say in Dublin."

Ever since Health Minister Michael Martin proposed the ban last year, surveys have shown most of Ireland's 3.9-million people—about 25 percent of whom are smokers—support the idea. It would be the most sweeping restriction on cigarette smoking imposed by any nation.

But enforcing the ban could be difficult.

Under the guidelines of the government's Office of Tobacco Control, pub owners can face fines of up to $4,000 per offense if they fail to make "all reasonable efforts" to deter smoking.

The guidelines specify pubs should display "no smoking" signs prominently at their entrances, bar areas and restrooms. Bar staff should tell smokers they're committing an offense, then, if they don't stop, refuse to serve them and ask them to leave.

If the customer refuses, the guidelines suggest calling the national police force.

Police officers have reacted with outrage.

"It's not a function for a police force at all. We haven't resources to deal with far more serious issues, never mind dealing with obstreperous smokers," said P.J. Stone of the officers' main union.

The ban's key enforcers are about 40 Health Department inspectors, who will be responsible for spotting violations in pubs and hotels. One hundred inspectors from the Health and Safety Authority—who monitor building sites, farms and other workplaces—will be asked to check for smoking employees, too.

The government has hired no additional inspectors to enforce the ban.

"There will be all-hours inspection," said Martin, who added: "Most people don't smoke, so there will be strong compliance."

Pubgoers predict that in tight-knit rural villages, pub owners will risk a fine rather than turn away familiar faces.

"This is a middle-class ban for city-center pubs in Dublin and a few other cities and towns," said Terry Rafferty, a retired bank manager and pub connoisseur from western County Mayo.

"In Dublin you've got huddles of health-conscious people, trendies. But out in the sticks, forget it—they're still very happily health-unconscious."

Joe Browne, president of the Vintners Federation, which represents 6,000 pubs outside Dublin, has pledged to help cover defense costs for pub owners taken to court for violating the ban.

Cigarette-machine vendors have imported more than 1-million tobacco-free "herbal" cigarettes, which, though carcinogenic, are not covered by the ban.

"Initially we expect there will be a novelty factor and we should sell quite a few on the first weekend," said Gerry Lawlor, spokesman for the Irish Cigarette Machine Operators' Association. "But it will probably fall off. I don't anticipate making a living out of it."

*Reprinted with permission of The Associated Press.*

2. Pull at least three quotes from the article and copy them in the left-hand column below.
3. Write a personal response to each quote in the right-hand column.
4. Post one of your quotes and personal responses on the class discussion board.
5. Respond to another classmate's response.

| Quote | Personal Response |
| --- | --- |
| Quote 1: | |
| Quote 2: | |
| Quote 3: | |

*Reflection Activity*

## *Rap a Rhyme: Make a Design*

**SURGEON GENERAL'S WARNING**: Quitting smoking now greatly reduces serious risks to your health.

**SURGEON GENERAL'S WARNING**: Smoking by pregnant women may result in fetal injury, premature birth, and low birth weight.

The above warnings can be found on cigarette boxes and give a clear explanation as to the dangers and effects of smoking. While the information in these warnings is important, they are oftentimes ignored.

### *Activity*

If you were an advertiser, how would you create a warning that would grab the attention of people your age that smoke? Using your creativity, write and design a warning label that would deter young people from smoking.

Be creative! Make it rap or rhyme! Create a neat design!

Post your ad to the discussion board.

Respond to another classmate's ad.

### *HIV Testing as Easy as 1-2-3!*

The Food and Drug Administration has recently approved a new product for HIV detection. The product, *OraQuick HIV-1/2* uses saliva and provides results in just 20 minutes. The traditional method requires a vial of blood and anywhere from 2 to 14 days to get results. Both methods can detect HIV antibodies as soon as six weeks after infection. Right now the test is mainly used as a preliminary screening tool, and requires verification if a positive result is detected.

## *Directions*

Read the article below. Then answer the questions that follow.

# HIV testing easy as swabbing spit

The FDA approves the test, which is more than 99 percent accurate and delivers results quickly without blood.

New York Times

The Food and Drug Administration on Friday approved the first HIV text that uses saliva rather than blood and delivers results in 20 minutes.

Public health officials hope the new test will encourage wider and more frequent testing. About 25 percent of all Americans carrying the AIDS virus do not know that they are infected, according to estimates by the Centers for Disease Control and Prevention. Around the world, that figure may be as high as 95 percent, according to the World Health Organization.

Although the test is as easy to use as a home-pregnancy kit and could eventually revolutionize HIV testing, the company, OraSure Technologies of Bethlehem, Pa., is not yet seeking approval for over-the-counter sales.

The test is more than 99 percent accurate and offers "more dignity, greater ease and no risk of transmission," said Michael Gausling, OraSure's president.

Calling the OraQuick HIV-1/2 test "another important option for people who might be afraid of a blood test," the secretary of health and human services, Tommy Thompson, announced the approval on Friday in a news conference in Washington, along with officials from the company, the FDA and the CDC.

The new test is "a very good thing," said Dr. Anthony S. Fauci, director of the National Institute of Allergy and Infectious Diseases and a prominent AIDS researcher. He

added, "It's extraordinary how many people don't come back for follow-up when they have to wait two weeks" for test results.

Typical HIV tests require a vial of blood and are sent to a laboratory that returns results in two to 14 days. Two years ago, the FDA approved an OraSure test that used only a drop of blood and gave results in 20 minutes; the company has since sold more than 500,000 of the tests, Gausling said. The new test uses the same technology and works as quickly, but with saliva, which is hundreds of times less infectious, and therefore less dangerous to the technician doing the test.

The test uses a plastic stick with a pad that is rubbed against the gums and placed in a vial of reagent solution. Within 20 minutes, if the result is positive, two reddish-purple lines appear on a small window on the handle.

The company says the new test can detect HIV antibodies as soon after infection as earlier tests—roughly six weeks, though the time for each person varies.

For now, it can be used only in certified laboratories, but Dr. Lester M. Crawford, the acting food and drug commissioner, "strongly urged" the company on Friday to apply for a waiver that would let the test be used in simpler settings, such as neighborhood clinics.

With such a waiver, Gausling said, "anyone with a seventh-grade education can administer the test if they can read instructions."

Fauci said he thought it was "almost certain" a waiver would be granted.

The test is for preliminary screening and must be confirmed with a more sophisticated test before treatment is begun, the company said. It is not approved for screening blood donations.

Shares of OraSure rose 19 percent on Friday, closing at $9.70.

Mark Harrington, executive director of the Treatment Action Group, which lobbies for better AIDS treatment, welcomed the new test but warned that it could be abused.

"What if they started using it on every immigrant at every airport?" he asked. "I'd see that as a violation of human rights."

He also worried that it would make it easier for the police or prison guards to give tests without consent, or for health authorities to test outside nightclubs or gay bars when patrons were too drunk to give legitimate consent or to be helped by counseling if they proved positive.

Saliva tests, including OraSure's, have been used for years in some developing countries where patients may be many miles from a clinic, said Dr. Basil Vareldzis, a Geneva AIDS specialist who helped write treatment guidelines for poor countries. "They're quite reliable, and much easier to use," he said.

They are also very useful for testing drug abusers, he said. Needle-sharing is the most common mode of transmission of human immunodeficiency virus in Russia, eastern Europe and some American cities.

"It's a big deal to get blood from an injection-drug user," Vareldzis said. "Some have veins that are all sclerosed. And former users in recovery can be really squeamish about being exposed to needles again. It's like giving a teaspoon of cough syrup with alcohol to a recovering alcoholic."

Several experts said the tests would be useful for anonymous surveillance to gauge the prevalence of disease. In South Africa in the late 1990s, a widely known study of AIDS among truck drivers used prostitutes at highway truck stops to get their clients to spit in jars, which were then put on ice and sent to a lab.

Although OraSure makes HIV tests for the life-insurance industry, Gausling said he doubted that insurance salesmen would want to give rapid tests because of the trauma that could ensue if a potential client proved positive.

1. How might this product benefit your own **personal development?**

2. How might this product benefit public health?

3. What possible abuses or violations of human rights might come from the use of this product?

4. Should there be any restrictions on the use of this product?

*Believe It or Not*

Get OFF the Diet Rollercoaster · · ·

Lose 10 lbs. **NOW!**

**FREE PRESCRIPTIONS!**

*No Prior Prescription Needed!*

**7-Minute Abs!**

*Shipped Overnight!*

*Lose Weight without Exercising!*

**No Doctor Appointments!** *On-Line Ordering!*

1. After reading the above headlines, what is the first thought that crosses your mind?

2. Have you ever fallen for a weight loss gimmick? If yes, which one and did it work?

3. What role does exercise and diet play in the maintenance of proper body weight and fat? Can you really lose weight without exercising?

# SCIENCE

Life science is a course designed to introduce you to the concepts and practical applications of the life sciences so that you will be informed citizens in an increasingly science and technology based society. It is critical to impart the knowledge necessary to form a morally and an ethically responsible opinion of the role science does and should play in shaping humanity now and in the future.

**At what age can we expect him to understand digital technology?**

From www.CartoonStock.com

"Look at each day as a chance to invest life into life. A chance to share your experience and deposit it into someone else's conscience. Each day is a chance to work miracles in the lives of others."

—*Jim Rohn*

*Reflection Activity*

## Weight Loss Fraudulence

The core value of **personal development** stresses the development of every person's mind, spirit, and body for a balanced life. In today's world of unlimited access to information via the Internet, we are constantly inundated with information concerning health and wellness. How do you know what is fact and what is fiction? Weight loss products and programs are just one example of the many products fraudulently advertised on the Internet and in the media.

## Directions

Visit the website www.healthyweightnetwork.com and click on *Identify Weight Loss Fraud & Quackery*. Then read the section titled *Guidelines for Identification*. Under each heading below write one example from the website that tells you how to identify fraudulent weight loss products and programs.

**Message:**

**Program:**

**Ingredients:**

**Mystique:**

**Method of Delivery:**

Explain how an activity such as this could help cultivate a sense of **personal development** in regard to your own health and wellness.

## On Your Own

Conduct a search of your own for a weight loss advertisement on the World Wide Web. Provide the URL address and evaluate the information provided using the same guidelines from above.

**URL Address:**

**Title of Site:**

**Message:**

**Program:**

**Ingredients:**

**Mystique:**

**Method of Delivery:**

# TECHNOLOGY

*Reflection Activity*

### Hocus Focus

### *Directions*

Respond to the following quotes from *The technology fix: The promise and reality of computers in our schools* by William D. Pflaum as they relate to the core value of **personal development.**

Computer use in general:

"Style over substance. Mechanics over meaning. These were the priorities I often observed in my school visits. Content was secondary; teacher and students focused on the *how,* not the *what*" (p. 141).

In regard to PowerPoint presentations:

"Technology advocates recommend that productivity tools be taught using relevant content, that the substance of the lesson should be relevant to the curriculum. Instead, the focus was almost exclusively on color, font selection, sound, animation, music selection, and other features" (p. 142).

Response:

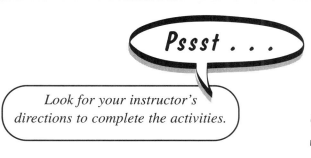

# CHAPTER 8

**Pssst . . .**

*Look for your instructor's directions to complete the activities.*

# RESPONSIBLE STEWARDSHIP

The Old English word *stigweard* from which we derive "steward" means house guardian and was associated with someone who cared for another's home and goods. As we use the term *responsible stewardship*, especially in a Benedictine context, it means the responsible and grateful use of all our resources, from the environment to the talents and gifts bestowed upon us. The practice of responsible stewardship is essential in caring for each other and the larger community. As the Benedictine Sisters of St. Scholastica state, responsible stewardship "is to be cultivated as a habit of loving concern."

> "Each one of you has received a special grace; so like good stewards responsible for all these different graces of God, put yourselves at the service of others."
> —*1 Peter 4:10*

## REFLECTION QUESTIONS

1. How are you a steward of the resources in your life?

2. What do you see as an obstacle in our society to **responsible stewardship?**

3. How is facing responsibility day after day a great adventure?

4. Define **responsible stewardship** in your own words.

First, take a moment to jot down what it means to be a responsible steward in society.

Then, preview the following website to determine the role of **responsible stewardship** in each scenario.

First go to 'Responsible Stewardship of Natural Resources and the Environment' from the U.S. Government Accounting Office website:

- http://www.gao.gov/sp/html/strobj17.html

1. What assumptions can you make regarding **responsible stewardship** from the government's point of view?

2. What is the basis for decision making about public resources?

3. How is the government fostering good stewardship of our public resources?

Next, go to the website for environmental design by Krech, O'Brien, Mueller & Wass, Inc.: "Sustainability and Energy: Responsible Stewardship" http://www.komw.com/sust_stew.htm

1. What does KOMW's mission statement say about their goals?

2. Overall, how does KOMW act as responsible stewards?

3. How is the concept of **responsible stewardship** connected to time management?

4. How will you be a **responsible steward** in planning your time wisely to have a successful college experience?

"I believe that all of us have the capacity for one adventure inside us, but great adventure is facing responsibility day after day."
—*William Gordon*

"Stewardship provides the people with an opportunity to live their way into a new kind of thinking rather than trying to think their way into a new kind of living."
—*Ministry of Money*

"Excellence is the gradual result of always striving to do better."
—*Pat Riley*

# SCIENCE

### *Invisible Principles*

1. Go to http://www.worldchlorine.com/stewardship

2. Read how *The World Chlorine Council* demonstrates their commitment to **responsible stewardship.**

3. Select a company, possible one you are currently working for, and identify five key principles your company could adopt for **responsible stewardship** in regard to its employees, the environment, and the community from which it resides.

   Principle 1

   Principle 2

   Principle 3

   Principle 4

   Principle 5

4. Post one of your principles on the class discussion board.

5. Read through several of the posted principles and respond to the postings of two of your classmates.

"Success on any major scale requires you to accept responsibility. In the final analysis, the one quality that all successful people have is the ability to take on responsibility."
—*Michael Korda*

# PHILOSOPHY/RELIGION

## *Destiny or Chance*

1. Do you agree or disagree with Calvin's final statement? Give your reasons.

2. How does Calvin's belief statement relate to the core value of **responsible stewardship?**

"BUT I <u>AM</u> RESPONSIBLE! WHEN YOUR LAMP GOT BROKEN, I WAS RESPONSIBLE. WHEN THE GOLDFISH DIED, I WAS RESPONSIBLE. WHEN MY BIKE GOT LEFT OUT IN THE RAIN."

From www.CartoonStock.com

"Work together for the benefit of all mankind.
Give assistance and kindness wherever needed.
Do what you know to be right.
Look after the well being of mind and body.
Dedicate a share of your efforts to the greater good.
Be truthful and honest at all times.
Take full responsibility for your actions."
—*Chief White Cloud*

Reflection Activity

### Plan Your Land

1. Visit *The Monastery of St. Gertrude's* website at http://www.stgertrudes.org

2. Click on *Stewardship of the Land.*

3. Read the Benedictine Sisters of Idaho's philosophy of land use.

4. Write your own philosophy of land use for the city/county/state in which you live below. First, begin your philosophy with a rich description of the area in which you live. Then describe which parts of the land are high on your list of preserving and offer a plan on how you and your community can keep this precious landscape from being spoiled.

***My Philosophy of Land Use for*** _____

(city/county/state)

5. Post your philosophy on the discussion board.

6. Respond to another classmate's land use philosophy.

### *I Declare!*

1.         Go to http://www.worldyouthalliance.org/declaration

2.         Read the *World Youth Alliance's* declaration on **responsible stewardship.**

3.         Write your own international declaration in regard to responsible stewardship below, giving specific examples of how you would accomplish it.

4. Post your declaration on the class discussion board.

5. Read through several other classmates' declarations. Discuss how they were alike. Discuss how they were different.

# CHAPTER 9

# INTEGRITY

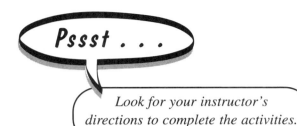

*Pssst . . .*

*Look for your instructor's directions to complete the activities.*

*The Latin word Integritas seems to have entered the language during the lifetime of Cicero. Its literal meaning is "the state of being untouched," thereby giving us the understanding that the person of integrity remains untainted by influences that would make life false. Benedict's Rule includes integrity as a center-point for living truthfully and espouses a simple life, lived with integrity.*

> "Be straight up!"
> —*D-Team*

> "Real integrity is doing the right thing, knowing that nobody's going to know whether you did it or not."
> —*Oprah Winfrey*

## REFLECTION QUESTIONS

1. Does your decision-making process vary from situation to situation? from person to person? Do these differences compromise your **integrity?**

2. What are the differences between acting morally and acting with **integrity?**

3. What is one occasion in your life where fear has caused you to act without **integrity?** What was the consequence?

4. Do you agree with Alice Miller's assessment of the person of **integrity?** Why or why not? (See the following page for quote.)

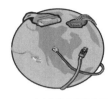

### Integrity in Taking Exams

Directions

1. Go to the University of Saint Thomas website below to determine the three best suggestions for taking tests.

    http://www.iss.stthomas.edu/studyguides/#Tests

2. Describe three suggestions you think are the most useful.

3. The section below speaks about emergency preparation—cramming. There are suggestions you might use when you do not manage your time adequately. Go to the website and complete the following questions.

    http://www.iss.stthomas.edu/studyguides/tstprpcrm.htm

4. Develop a chart that compares and contrasts the two lists of suggestions.

### Integrity and the Business World

1. Now, take a moment to reflect on your definition of **integrity.** Can you add to your definition? How does the value of **integrity** apply to test taking? What are some issues that are common to **integrity** and test preparation?

2. **Integrity** is, of course, an integral part of the business world. Go to the following websites of two large successful companies:
   - http://www.ge.com/en/commitment/social/integrity/
   - http://www.integrity-interactive.com/welcome.htm

3. How is the value of **integrity** important to the company image and to its goals?

4. Why should a company want to promote the value of **integrity?**

5. How is the value of **integrity** in test taking related to these companies' visions and/or goals?

6. Here is a website of a company that specializes in selling tests that measure the **integrity** of workers:
   http://www.assessmentspecialists.com/step.html.

7. After reading the information, what is your response to such a venture?

8. How would you feel about having your employer try to measure your level of **integrity?**

9. Team up with another person in class and debate whether a company should measure **integrity** before hiring. What about after hiring?

"Integrity needs no rules."
—*Albert Camus*

"A single lie destroys a whole reputation of integrity."
—*Baltasar Gracian*

"Integrity without knowledge is weak and useless, and knowledge without integrity is dangerous and dreadful."
—*Samuel Johnson*

"The integrity of the game is everything."
—*Peter Ueberroth*

"It's more important to do the right thing than to do things right."
—*Peter Drucker*

# ENGLISH

### Note and Quote It

The value of **integrity** includes many related concepts and terms: ethics, authenticity, sincerity, honesty, or staying true to a code of behavior. All of these concepts relate to decisions that we make that influence the kind of people we become. Some of what we discover about ourselves can be seen in the kind of writing we produce. In writing, we strive to reflect our thoughts clearly, honestly, and respectfully and credit those other thinkers and writers to whom we are indebted for their ideas and inspiration. Writing research papers is a common part of college life. Yet, if you do not take great care with the research process, you may be accused of plagiarism, a form of academic dishonesty. Simply put, plagiarism is representing the words or ideas of someone else as your own. Failing to organize your sources, take careful notes that identify sources, or clearly mark direct quotations with quotation marks, can all result in plagiarism. You may start a paper too late, and in the panic that ensues, neglect to properly cite sources. You may copy huge chunks of text directly from a source without citing it, or you may fail to distinguish your own ideas from your sources. Despite your protestations that you are innocent of academic dishonesty, the charge still stands, for intention has little to do with guilt.

It's best to get acquainted with some basics about maintaining academic honesty early in your studies. You can find helpful information to avoid plagiarism in all sorts of sources from your grammar handbooks, your instructors' classrooms, or a learning resource center to thousands of online writing labs. Even with all of that preparation and reading, however, you may still find yourself in a situation where you have plagiarized. Often, this means that you have placed yourself in one of many *high risk* situations which increase the chances of your plagiarizing on an assignment. Therefore, it's wise to be aware of some common high-risk situations that may set you up for unintentional plagiarism, a failure of academic integrity. For some very useful advice, carefully read the following excerpted tips from Harvard University's, *Writing with Sources: A Guide for Harvard Students*. (The more detailed version of this can be found in the appendix at the end of your book.)

## HOW TO AVOID HIGH-RISK SITUATIONS

1. Don't leave written work until the last minute.

2. Don't use secondary sources for a paper unless you are asked or explicitly allowed to.

3. Don't rely exclusively on a single secondary source for information or opinion in a research paper. If you do, your paper may be less well-informed and balanced that it should be, and moreover you may be lulled into plagiarizing the source. Using several different sources forces you to step back and evaluate or triangulate them.

From Siobhan Herkert

4. When you take notes, take pains to distinguish the words and thoughts of the source from your own, so you don't mistake them for your own later. Adopt these habits in particular:

- Either summarize radically or quote exactly, always using quotation marks when you quote. Don't take notes by loosely copying out source material and simply changing a few words.

- When you take a note or quote from a source, jot the author's name and page number beside each note you take (don't simply jot down ideas anonymously) and record the source's publication data on that same page in your notes, to save yourself having to dig it up as you are rushing to finish your paper. Save even more time by recording this information in the same order and format you will use for listing references on your final draft.

- Take or transcribe your notes on sources in a separate word-processing file, not in the file in which you are drafting your paper. And keep these files separate throughout the writing of the paper, bringing in source material from your notes only as needed.

5. Take notes actively, not passively. Don't just copy down the source's words or ideas, but record your own reactions and reflections, questions, and hunches. Note where you find yourself resisting or doubting or puzzling over what a source says; jot down possible arguments or observations you might want to make. These will provide starting points when you turn to write your paper; and they will help keep you from feeling overwhelmed by your sources or your notes.

6. Don't try to sound more sophisticated or learned than you are.

7. If you feel stuck, confused, or panicked about time, or if you are having problems in your life and can't concentrate, let your instructor know.

8. Don't ask to borrow another student's paper if you are stuck or running late with an assignment. Reading it will probably discourage or panic rather than inspire you, and it may tempt you to plagiarize. Instead, ask the student to help you brainstorm some of your own ideas.

9. Don't write a paper from borrowed notes, since you have no way of knowing the source or the words and ideas. They may, for example, come directly from a book or lecture, or from a book discussed in lecture.

10. Don't do the actual writing of a paper with another student, or split the writing between you, unless you have explicit permission. Even if you collaborate on a project, you're expected to express the results in your own words.

11. Don't submit to one class a paper or even sections of a paper, that you have submitted or will submit to another class, without first getting the written permission of both instructors.

12. Always back up your work on diskette, and make a hard copy each time you end a long working session or finish a paper.

" I never graduated from college. I got caught cheating on my ethics exam."

From www.CartoonStock.com

## Words, Words, Words

Now that you have carefully reflected on the high-risk situations, reread Chapter 2 in your book on values education. Follow Steps 4 and 5 from "How to Avoid High-Risk Situations" and

1. take notes from one section of the chapter, following the steps in #4.
2. take "active" notes from the same section of the chapter, following the steps in #5.

As you actively take notes, remember to record your questions, reactions, or observations on the passage. In short, critically THINK about the passage rather than simply copying parts of it to your own notes. Use the notetaking sheet below to help you use the strategy of active note taking.

# ACTIVE NOTETAKING SHEET

| | |
|---|---|
| **SOURCE** | |
| **PAGE NUMBERS** | |
| **QUOTE** _____ | |
| **PARAPHRASE** _____ | |
| **REFLECTIONS** | |
| **REACTIONS** | |
| **QUESTIONS** | |

*Reflection Activity*

### Your Words or Mine

One way of sharing information from a source is to paraphrase it, using your own words. In short, a **paraphrase** is simply a restatement of a passage of text. However, paraphrasing can be tricky for beginning writers. Oddly enough, many students believe unless they are directly quoting a source, they do not have to credit it. Nothing could be further from the truth. Remember that maintaining academic integrity in writing includes giving credit to your sources. Period. That means that whether you alter the wording of a passage or use direct quotes, you are still depending upon another person for your information.

If you paraphrase an entire passage or paragraph, you should try to keep to the organization of the original and leave out the editorializing. For example, reread the paragraph above that begins this section on paraphrasing. Then read the paraphrase of the original paragraph below:

> Paraphrasing is a simple way to give information to your readers. A paraphrase is a restatement of the original language of a text using your own words. Although many students do not recognize that they must give credit to a source whether or not they are using the direct words of the original, they must give credit to a source when they paraphrase and when they quote a source directly.

Notice that the paraphrased version keeps to the general pattern of the original, makes the same basic points, and uses different wording. Because the information comes from another source, however, you must document the original source. Remember also that if you do use any wording from the original, you must always include quotation marks around exact wording as well as provide a citation for the source.

Although we won't go into the various documentation styles that are available to you here, you should ask your instructors if they prefer a particular documentation style when you submit your papers. Various associations in disciplines of study determine certain rules for documenting sources and writing reference pages. Students writing papers in the humanities, for example, commonly use the Modern Language Association's form, referred to as "MLA." Those in the social sciences usually use the American Psychological Association's form, referred to as "APA," while those in business more commonly use the Chicago Manual of Style or the "CMS" form. So always find out what documentation style you should use in your assignments.

Now let's try to practice some of the principles discussed in this section.

### Directions

The following passage is taken from Richard Stengel's book *You're Too Kind: A Brief History of Flattery,* published by Simon and Schuster in 2000. In it, Stengel amusingly and informatively outlines the history of flattery, from the elaborate and refined use of flattery by ancient peoples to rather talented flatterers of our own time. In Chapter 2, "You Can't Take It with You," Stengel discusses the pharaoh Ramses II and his particular penchant for self-flattery:

As a pharaoh, Ramses II was unmatched in terms of vanity construction. Ramses ruled for an estimated sixty-seven years and had a mania for construction. He built a series of temples for himself at Abu Simbel that one entered by passing through two sixty-seven foot statues of himself carved out of the side of the mountain. This would be like Teddy Roosevelt's deciding to dedicate Mt. Rushmore all to himself. Just so no one could ever mistake who is buried there, the two statues of Ramses at Abu Simbel show him seated, while the figures of his immediate family come about halfway up to his knees.

For the pharaohs, the tombs were advertisements that signified the importance of their occupants. In the Valley of Kings, where the mountainside is honeycombed with tombs, the pharaoh and his court inscribed their accomplishments on the sides of their tombs. These inscriptions on the outside of the temples were permanent billboards touting the greatness of those buried within. The builders and artisans were like a resident staff of press agents for the pharaoh, touting his image, polishing his record (58–59).

> Ramses regarded himself as a king among kings, a warrior among warriors. But his military fame rests less on his own exploits than on his own words. His actual military record is modest, but accounts of his valor and courage were inscribed on the walls of every major temple of his era. Like every pharaoh, he never failed to claim success where failure had occurred, never hesitated to invent a victory where nothing at all may have happened. There are no newspapers or television reports to contradict him. For Ramses, the first draft of history was carved in stone. Ramses outdid the other pharaohs not so much in battles but in sheer wall space. Pictures depict him as a giant wiping out whole divisions of enemies. One temple says that the portrayal of the defeat of Egypt's enemies is meant to be "a lesson for a million generations." In ancient Egypt, the word was father to the deed. If it was said or written, it had happened. (Ramses did know how to flatter his wife, though. The inscription above the entrance above her temple reads, "SHE FOR WHOM THE SUN DOTH SHINE" (58–59)).

## Directions

1. Write a paraphrase of one of the paragraphs from Stengel's writing, keeping in mind the guidelines we have established for proper paraphrasing. Post your paraphrase to the class discussion board.

2. Using the passage from Stengel's book, identify three points that Stengel makes about Ramses and ancient temples. Then create a paragraph of your own in which you use those points and properly give credit to Stengel's ideas by both quoting directly and using your own words. Follow your instructor's directions on which documentation style you should use for this exercise.

*Reflection Activity*

## *The Moral of the Story Is . . .*

One of the most common ways children of all ages learn lessons is through the form of the fable. In the fable, animals are commonly used to represent various virtues and foibles of humans. Through the legacy of *Aesop's Fables,* we have become familiar with some of these representative types: the fox has become equated with cunning, the owl with wisdom, and the turtle with deliberation. Unlike the fairy tale, which may have more complex meanings, symbols, and images, the fable is a straightforward story, which explicitly teaches a moral lesson. Many writers since Aesop have reinvented the fable, making its images and messages more suited to their own time. The nineteenth-century American writer Ambrose Bierce, for example, wrote a series of fables, which revealed his own cynicism about life while humorist James Thurber revisited the fable to create "fables for our time."

Read the Aesop's fable below to re-familiarize yourself with the form.

## The Fox and the Monkey

A Fox and a Monkey were traveling together on the same road. As they journeyed, they passed through a cemetery full of monuments.

"All these monuments which you see," said the Monkey, "are erected in honor of my ancestors, who were in their day freedmen and citizens of great renown."

The Fox replied, "You have chosen a most appropriate subject for your falsehoods, as I am sure none of your ancestors will be able to contradict you."

Moral: A false tale often betrays itself.

## *Directions*

Now, using one of the statements below about lying as the moral, write a fable of your own which illustrates the moral. Update your fable, using images and scenes from contemporary life, but make sure that animals stand-in for the virtues or vices you want to illustrate:

1. Lying to ourselves is more deeply ingrained than lying to others (Fyodor Dostoevsky, 1821–1881).

2. The liar's punishment . . . is that he cannot believe anyone else (George Bernard Shaw (1856–1950).

3. Post your fable to the class discussion board.

4. Feel free to respond to other classmates' fables.

My Fable

# SCIENCE

## Marching through the Method

Upon entering a general education science course, the process of 'scientific inquiry' is seldom simple and usually varies widely, depending on the case under study. Even so, you are so often convinced that all scientists march through five basic, sequential steps as they "do science." These steps are called the scientific method; unfortunately however, when asked to distinguish between biased results and unbiased results, science and pseudoscience, your knowledge of the scientific method provides little guidance. This activity is intended to frame the scientific method within the core value of **integrity**. As a class you will discuss traits common to all scientific work, for example, observations and experiments, results that anyone can reproduce, theories that make testable predictions, logical and consistent reasoning, and peer review.

1. Relate the core value of **integrity** to the field of science.

2. Can a scientist have personal **integrity** even if his or her science lacks **integrity?**

3. Go to the Internet to find information on other "scientific" studies. Find initial reports of cold fusion by two chemists at the University of Utah, studies of UFO's and alien contacts, and/or evidence presented for the theory of creationism. Post your information to the class discussion board.

   a. Website you visited: http://www. _____

   b. Is the work on which you are reporting consistent with accepted scientific methods? How? How not?

   c. Does it have **integrity?** Why? Why not?

   d. Are the individuals reporting the work of people of **integrity?**

   e. What role does **integrity** play in the way we 'do science', that is, the "scientific method?"

   f. How is the **integrity** of science ensured, in the long term, by the method itself?

# SOCIOLOGY

### *Through the Looking Glass*

When we think of the word **integrity,** we usually think of wholeness; having all the pieces together; honesty, trustworthiness, promises, but perhaps more importantly, know what promises to make.

**Bottom line:** Mean what you say, say what you mean, and do what you say.

## Questions

1. How consistent are you with what you say, what you mean, and what you do?

2. Are you a promise keeper or breaker?

3. What are the positive and negative experiences as a promise keeper? a promise breaker?

4. From what sources (family, friends, schools, other institutions) have you experienced promises being kept or broken?

5. Tell about one experience of a kept or broken promise.

6. How has this affected your sense of integrity or trust in others?

7. How has kept or broken promises affected you?

8. How does keeping or breaking promises affect your decision to be a person of **integrity** or trustworthiness?

*Reflection Activity*

### *Into Temptation*

According to sociologist, James Henslin (1999) . . .

Research ethics requires openness (sharing findings with the scientific community), honesty, and truth. This clearly forbids the falsification of results, as well as plagiarism—that is stealing someone else's work. Another basic ethical guideline is that research subjects should not be harmed by the research. Ethics also requires the sociologists to protect the anonymity of people who provide information, which is embarrassing, or otherwise harmful to them. Finally, it generally is considered unethical for researchers to misrepresent themselves (p. 136).

Other common principles of ethics research are:

Informed consent: Researchers need to ensure voluntary participation therefore; one needs to obtain consent from the research participants or parents in case of children.
Debriefing: Researchers inform the research participants exactly why they are doing the research.

### *Questions*

1. What are the temptations to conducting unethical research? Give examples.

2. Identify how you could change these unethical examples into ways of conducting research with **integrity.**

### Internet Activity

1. Search on the Internet for a sociological research article by accessing search engines such as www.yahoo.com or www.excite.com. Type in "sociology research article."

2. Choose an article that interests you and analyze the integrity or trustworthiness of the research.

3. Did the researcher abide by the code of ethics?

4. Did the researcher represent the results truthfully?

**"I'll be in touch if we need somebody with integrity."**

From www.CartoonStock.com

# TECHNOLOGY

Reflection Activity

### *Deciphering the Code: Integrity and Technology*

The information workforce of tomorrow provides fertile ground for you to connect your new knowledge with the value of **integrity.** You enroll in a course to develop specific skills, understand how information is acquired, and learn more about the asynchronous and synchronous world.

You become what Turkle (1984) calls *"intrepid explorers"* in testing your skills in a context appropriate to your career goals. For example, you may be required to participate in a listserv with peers to discuss information and relate relative literature or ideas for further research. You are constantly reminded not to "spam" or send unwanted messages to others not working on the same project. More than likely, you set up or respond to surveys on a web page, use chat rooms, message boards, and post responses to assignments. Your **integrity** is challenged when faced with issues such as copyright, security, and plagiarism.

### *Directions*

Read the excerpts below from *Implementing the Seven Principles: Technology as Lever* by Chickering and Ehrmann (1997) and answer the questions that follow.

1. Frequent student-faculty contact in and out of the classroom is a *most* important factor in student motivation and involvement.

   *Do you find this factor hard to achieve as an online learner? Explain your answer.*
   *What do you do when you have a question or concern about a class or an assignment?*

2. Study groups, collaborative learning, group problem solving, and discussion of assignments can all be dramatically strengthened through communication tools provided on-line.

   *Do you consider technology a 24/7 solution? Support your answer with details.*

3. Feedback is constantly reinforcing. Computers can record and analyze personal and professional performances.

   *How do you prefer to receive feedback on assignments?*

4. To support classroom research, computers can record student participation and interaction and help document student time on task, especially as related to student performance.

   *Discuss whether recording your participation and interaction via technology is beneficial to your learning?*

5. Students feel stimulated by knowing their finished work will be "published" on the World Wide Web.

   *What are some of the dangers of having your work published on the World Wide Web?*

6. Different students bring different talents and styles to college. Brilliant students in a seminar might be all thumbs in a lab or studio; students rich in hands-on experience may not do so well with theory. Students need opportunities to show their talents and learn in ways that work for them.

   *As an online learner, do you agree that technology supports opportunities for you to demonstrate your knowledge? Explain your response.*

## *Asynchronous or Synchronous: Integrity Communicated*

When using the Internet you confront your morals and values through both asynchronous and synchronous assignments. So, working with a partner, list ways you maintain your **integrity** when using technology? Post your response to the class discussion board.

*Activities for Integrating Values for Online Learners*

## *Questions*

1. How does **integrity** fit into your definition of using technology?

2. What would the technological field be like if **integrity** was missing?

3. Why is **integrity** essential in using technology?

4. Design a company policy for the use of technology by all employees. Which values will you incorporate?

5. In learning by connecting to the Internet, how do you assure **integrity** in the learning environment? Is **integrity** absolutely necessary for learning?

6. What is the value in the use of turnitin.com? Do you think it should be required in every class? If so, why? If not, why not?

*Upload? Download? Just Say NO!*

## Pirates of the Internet

Ahoy! Six months and a $7,000 charge for uploading films onto the Internet? It's happening, as federal prosecutors start stomping digital buccaneers.

Last June a friend working on an ad campaign for *The Hulk* gave Kerry Gonzalez a copy of the movie before it even opened. Gonzalez, a 25-year-old film buff, uploaded it onto the Internet. By the time he clicked "send," he says, "I started having nightmares about the FBI coming to get me. I'd wake up in the middle of the night and feel guilty about the whole thing."

Good guess. A week later Gonzalez's pal phoned to say FBI agents had come to the ad agency to question him. Panicked, Gonzalez, an insurance underwriter from Hamilton Township, N.J., turned himself in. On June 5 he pleaded guilty in a Manhattan federal court to making an unauthorized copy of the film and uploading it. Although Gonzalez avoided a potential three years in prison and a $250,000 fine, he was sentenced to six months house arrest and ordered to pay $7,000 in fines and restitution. "This has ruined my life," he says.

If the Motion Picture Association of America (MPAA) has its way, others may soon be as rueful as Gonzalez. The film industry's advocacy group is on a crusade against uploaders and downloaders and has not ruled out lawsuits similar to those the music industry filed last September. If the MPAA does decide to make legal action a priority, "we will prosecute with great speed," says president Jack Valenti. Movie studios lose more than $3.5 billion.

### Questions

1. What do you think of Gonzalez's decision to turn himself in?

2. Relate Gonzalez's decision to our core value of **integrity.**

3. Have you ever downloaded a movie or music from the Internet?

   Did you know that it was illegal?

   If you answered yes, would you continue to download in the future or do you feel differently about it now?

4. Whether you answered yes or no, what does it say about your own integrity?

5. Do you think people maintain their **integrity** out of fear of being caught? Explain your answer.

# CHAPTER 10

# FUSING IT ALL TOGETHER

### Sees the World

Well, you've done a lot of work on values, and, hopefully, during the process you have generated some thoughts of your own about how values inform our lives and influence who we are as human beings. Early in the book, you were asked to do the *Global You* activity to think more fully about values that match your particular age group. Now let's see how the Nexters view the world around them.

### Directions

1. Look at the following table to see how the different generations view the world. After examining these world views fill in the far right column for the *Nexters* generation. How do they view the world?

|  | **Veterans** | **Boomers** | **Gen Xers** | **Nexters** |
|---|---|---|---|---|
| **Outlook** | Practical | Optimistic | Skeptical | |
| **Media Impact** | Radio | Television | Computer | |
| **Work Ethic** | Dedicated | Driven | Balanced | |
| **View of Authority** | Respectful | Love/Hate | Unimpressed | |
| **Leadership by** | Hierarchy | Consensus | Competence | |
| **Relationships** | Personal sacrifice | Personal incorrectness | Reluctance to Commit | |
| **Turnoffs** | Vulgarity | Political Incorrectness | Cliché, hype | |

*Activity adapted from: Stringer, D., & Cassidy, P. A. (2003). 52 Activities for exploring values differences. Yarmouth, ME: Nicholas Brealey Publishing (p. 53–55).*

2. Compare your answers to those that your instructor sends you as the generally accepted views of that generation. Record those views on the lines below.

Outlook _____

Media Impact _____

Work Ethic _____

View of Authority _____

Leadership by _____

Relationships _____

Turnoffs _____

3. How closely do the views that you identified match with those supplied by your instructor?

4. How many of your world views belonged to only one group?

5. What have you learned about yourself and how you view others?

*Choose It, Fuse It, Use It, or Lose It!*

*Choose It!*

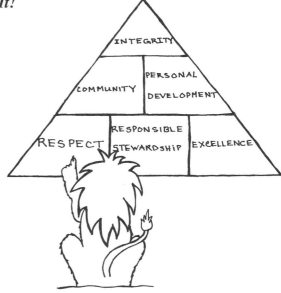

From Siobhan Herkert

Circle the values that you hold in highest esteem. E-mail your choices to a classmate.

**Core Values:** Excellence, Community, Respect, Personal Development, Responsible Stewardship, Integrity

*Fuse It!*

How can you best implement these values in your life?

From Siobhan Herkert

## Use It!

How will you live these values in a way you hadn't thought about before?

From Siobhan Herkert

## Lose It!

How would your life be different if values had no meaning?

From Siobhan Herkert

## Outline of Values by Discipline

| Discipline: | Values: |
|---|---|
| **English** | Respect, Integrity |
| **Fine Arts** | Community, Personal Development |
| **Mathematics** | Respect, Excellence |
| **Personal Wellness** | Personal Development |
| **Philosophy/Religion** | Community, Excellence, Responsible Stewardship |
| **Science** | Integrity, Personal Development, Responsible Stewardship, Respect |
| **Social Sciences** | |
| History | Community, Respect |
| Psychology | Community, Respect |
| Sociology | Community, Respect, Integrity, Responsible Stewardship |
| **Technology** | Integrity, Personal Development |

# ETHICAL PRINCIPLES OF PSYCHOLOGISTS AND CODE OF CONDUCT
## 2002 (APA, 2002)

# APA Ethics Code 2002

## INTRODUCTION AND APPLICABILITY

The American Psychological Association's (APA's) Ethical Principles of Psychologists and Code of Conduct (hereinafter referred to as the Ethics Code) consists of an Introduction, a Preamble, five General Principles (A–E), and specific Ethical Standards. The Introduction discusses the intent, organization, procedural considerations, and scope of application of the Ethics Code. The Preamble and General Principles are aspirational goals to guide psychologists toward the highest ideals of psychology. Although the Preamble and General Principles are not themselves enforceable rules, they should be considered by psychologists in arriving at an ethical course of action. The Ethical Standards set forth enforceable rules for conduct as psychologists. Most of the Ethical Standards are written broadly, in order to apply to psychologists in varied roles, although the application of an Ethical Standard may vary depending on the context. The Ethical Standards are not exhaustive. The fact that a given conduct is not specifically addressed by an Ethical Standard does not mean that it is necessarily either ethical or unethical.

This Ethics Code applies only to psychologists' activities that are part of their scientific, educational, or professional roles as psychologists. Areas covered include but are not limited to the clinical, counseling, and school practice of psychology; research; teaching; supervision of trainees; public service; policy development; social intervention; development of assessment instruments; conducting assessments; educational counseling; organizational consulting; forensic activities; program design and evaluation; and administration. This Ethics Code applies to these activities across a variety of contexts, such as in person, postal, telephone, internet, and other electronic transmissions. These activities shall be distinguished from the purely private conduct of psychologists, which is not within the purview of the Ethics Code.

Membership in the APA commits members and student affiliates to comply with the standards of the APA Ethics Code and to the rules and procedures used to enforce them. Lack of awareness or misunderstanding of an Ethical Standard is not itself a defense to a charge of unethical conduct.

The procedures for filing, investigating, and resolving complaints of unethical conduct are described in the current Rules and Procedures of the APA Ethics Committee. APA may impose sanctions on its members for violations of the standards of the Ethics Code, including termination of APA membership, and may notify other bodies and individuals of its actions. Actions that violate the standards of the Ethics Code may also lead to the imposition of sanctions on psychologists or students whether or not they are APA members by bodies other than APA, including state psychological associations, other professional groups, psychology boards, other state or federal agencies, and payors for health services. In addition, APA may take action against a member after his or her conviction of a felony, expulsion or suspension from an affiliated state psychological association, or suspension or loss of licensure. When the sanction to be imposed by APA is less than expulsion, the 2001 Rules and Procedures do not guarantee an opportunity for an in-person hearing, but generally provide that complaints will be resolved only on the basis of a submitted record.

The Ethics Code is intended to provide guidance for psychologists and standards of professional conduct that can be applied by the APA and by other bodies that choose to adopt them. The Ethics Code is not intended to be a basis of civil liability. Whether a psychologist has violated the Ethics Code standards does not by itself determine whether the psychologist is legally liable in a court action, whether a contract is enforceable, or whether other legal consequences occur.

The modifiers used in some of the standards of this Ethics Code (e.g., *reasonably, appropriate, potentially*) are included in the standards when they would (1) allow professional judgment on the part of psychologists, (2) eliminate injustice or inequality that would occur without the modifier, (3) ensure applicability across the broad range of activities conducted by psychologists, or (4) guard against a set of rigid rules that might be quickly outdated. As used in this Ethics Code, the term *reasonable* means the prevailing professional judgment of psychologists engaged in similar activities in similar circumstances, given the knowledge the psychologist had or should have had at the time.

In the process of making decisions regarding their professional behavior, psychologists must consider this Ethics Code in addition to applicable laws and psychology board regulations. In applying the Ethics Code to their professional work, psychologists may consider other materials and guidelines that have been adopted or endorsed by scientific and professional psychological organizations and the dictates of their own conscience, as well as consult with others within the field. If this Ethics Code establishes a higher standard of conduct than is required by law, psychologists must meet the higher ethical standard. If psychologists' ethical responsibilities conflict with law, regulations, or other governing legal authority, psychologists make known their commitment to this Ethics Code and take steps to resolve the conflict in a responsible manner. If the conflict is unresolvable via such means, psychologists may adhere to the requirements of the law, regulations, or other governing authority in keeping with basic principles of human rights.

# PREAMBLE

Psychologists are committed to increasing scientific and professional knowledge of behavior and people's understanding of themselves and others and to the use of such knowledge to improve the condition of individuals, organizations, and society. Psychologists respect and protect civil and human rights and the central importance of freedom of inquiry and expression in research, teaching, and publication. They strive to help the public in developing informed judgments and choices concerning human behavior. In doing so, they perform many roles, such as researcher, educator, diagnostician, therapist, supervisor, consultant, administrator, social interventionist, and expert witness. This Ethics Code provides a common set of principles and standards upon which psychologists build their professional and scientific work.

This Ethics Code is intended to provide specific standards to cover most situations encountered by psychologists. It has as its goals the welfare and protection of the individuals and groups with whom psychologists work and the education of members, students, and the public regarding ethical standards of the discipline.

The development of a dynamic set of ethical standards for psychologists' work-related conduct requires a personal commitment and lifelong effort to act ethically; to encourage ethical behavior by students, supervisees, employees, and colleagues; and to consult with others concerning ethical problems.

# GENERAL PRINCIPLES

This section consists of General Principles. General Principles, as opposed to Ethical Standards, are aspirational in nature. Their intent is to guide and inspire psychologists toward the very highest ethical ideals of the profession. General Principles, in contrast to Ethical Standards, do not represent obligations and should not form the basis for imposing sanctions. Relying upon General Principles for either of these reasons distorts both their meaning and purpose.

## Principle A: Beneficence and Nonmaleficence

Psychologists strive to benefit those with whom they work and take care to do no harm. In their professional actions, psychologists seek to safeguard the welfare and rights of those with whom they interact professionally and other affected persons, and the welfare of animal subjects of research. When conflicts occur among psychologists' obligations or concerns, they attempt to resolve these conflicts in a responsible fashion that avoids or minimizes harm. Because psychologists' scientific and professional judgments and actions may affect the lives of others, they are alert to and guard against personal, financial, social, organizational, or political factors that might lead to misuse of their influence. Psychologists strive to be aware of the possible effect of their own physical and mental health on their ability to help those with whom they work.

## Principle B: Fidelity and Responsibility

Psychologists establish relationships of trust with those with whom they work. They are aware of their professional and scientific responsibilities to society and to the specific communities in which they work. Psychologists uphold professional standards of conduct, clarify their professional roles and obligations, accept appropriate responsibility for their behavior, and seek to manage conflicts of interest that could lead to exploitation or harm. Psychologists consult with, refer to, or cooperate with other professionals and institutions to the extent needed to serve the best interests of those with whom they work. They are concerned about the ethical compliance of their colleagues' scientific and professional conduct. Psychologists strive to contribute a portion of their professional time for little or no compensation or personal advantage.

## Principle C: Integrity

Psychologists seek to promote accuracy, honesty, and truthfulness in the science, teaching, and practice of psychology. In these activities psychologists do not steal, cheat, or engage in fraud, subterfuge, or intentional misrepresentation of fact. Psychologists strive to keep their promises and to avoid unwise or unclear commitments. In situations in which deception may be ethically justifiable to maximize benefits and minimize harm, psychologists have a serious obligation to consider the need for, the possible consequences of, and their responsibility to correct any resulting mistrust or other harmful effects that arise from the use of such techniques.

## Principle D: Justice

Psychologists recognize that fairness and justice entitle all persons to access to and benefit from the contributions of psychology and to equal quality in the processes, procedures, and services being conducted by psychologists. Psychologists exercise reasonable judgment and take precautions to ensure that their potential biases, the boundaries of their competence, and the limitations of their expertise do not lead to or condone unjust practices.

## Principle E: Respect for People's Rights and Dignity

Psychologists respect the dignity and worth of all people, and the rights of individuals to privacy, confidentiality, and self-determination. Psychologists are aware that special safeguards may be necessary to protect the rights and welfare of persons or communities whose vulnerabilities impair autonomous decision making. Psychologists are aware of and respect cultural, individual, and role differences, including those based on age, gender, gender identity, race, ethnicity, culture, national origin, religion, sexual orientation, disability, language, and socioeconomic status and consider these factors when working with members of such groups. Psychologists try to eliminate the effect on their work of biases based on those factors, and they do not knowingly participate in or condone activities of others based upon such prejudices.

# ETHICAL STANDARDS

## 1. Resolving Ethical Issues

### 1.01 Misuse of Psychologists' Work

If psychologists learn of misuse or misrepresentation of their work, they take reasonable steps to correct or minimize the misuse or misrepresentation.

### 1.02 Conflicts Between Ethics and Law, Regulations, or Other Governing Legal Authority

If psychologists' ethical responsibilities conflict with law, regulations, or other governing legal authority, psychologists make known their commitment to the Ethics Code and take steps to resolve the conflict. If the conflict is unresolvable via such means, psychologists may adhere to the requirements of the law, regulations, or other governing legal authority.

### 1.03 Conflicts Between Ethics and Organizational Demands

If the demands of an organization with which psychologists are affiliated or for whom they are working conflict with this Ethics Code, psychologists clarify the nature of the conflict, make known their commitment to the Ethics Code, and to the extent feasible, resolve the conflict in a way that permits adherence to the Ethics Code.

### 1.04 Informal Resolution of Ethical Violations

When psychologists believe that there may have been an ethical violation by another psychologist, they attempt to resolve the issue by bringing it to the attention of that individual, if an informal resolution appears appropriate and the intervention does not violate any confidentiality rights that may be involved. (See also Standards 1.02, Conflicts Between Ethics and Law, Regulations, or Other Governing Legal Authority, and 1.03, Conflicts Between Ethics and Organizational Demands.)

### 1.05 Reporting Ethical Violations

If an apparent ethical violation has substantially harmed or is likely to substantially harm a person or organization and is not appropriate for informal resolution under Standard 1.04, Informal Resolution of Ethical Violations, or is not resolved properly in that fashion, psychologists take further action appropriate to the situation. Such action might include referral to state or national committees on professional ethics, to state licensing boards, or to the appropriate institutional authorities. This standard does not apply when an intervention would violate confidentiality rights or when psychologists have been retained to review the work of another psychologist whose professional conduct is in question. (See also Standard 1.02, Conflicts Between Ethics and Law, Regulations, or Other Governing Legal Authority.)

### 1.06 Cooperating With Ethics Committees

Psychologists cooperate in ethics investigations, proceedings, and resulting requirements of the APA or any affiliated state psychological association to which they belong. In doing so, they address any confidentiality issues. Failure to cooperate is itself an ethics violation. However, making a request for deferment of adjudication of an ethics complaint pending the outcome of litigation does not alone constitute noncooperation.

### 1.07 Improper Complaints

Psychologists do not file or encourage the filing of ethics complaints that are made with reckless disregard for or willful ignorance of facts that would disprove the allegation.

### 1.08 Unfair Discrimination Against Complainants and Respondents

Psychologists do not deny persons employment, advancement, admissions to academic or other programs, tenure, or promotion, based solely upon their having made or their being the subject of an ethics complaint. This does not preclude taking action based upon the outcome of such proceedings or considering other appropriate information.

## 2. Competence

### 2.01 Boundaries of Competence

(a) Psychologists provide services, teach, and conduct research with populations and in areas only within the boundaries of their competence, based on their education, training, supervised experience, consultation, study, or professional experience.

(b) Where scientific or professional knowledge in the discipline of psychology establishes that an understanding of factors associated with age, gender, gender identity, race, ethnicity, culture, national origin, religion, sexual orientation, disability, language, or socioeconomic status is essential for effective implementation of their services or research, psychologists have or obtain the training, experience, consultation, or supervision necessary to ensure the competence of their services, or they make appropriate referrals, except as provided in Standard 2.02, Providing Services in Emergencies.

(c) Psychologists planning to provide services, teach, or conduct research involving populations, areas, techniques, or technologies new to them undertake relevant education, training, supervised experience, consultation, or study.

(d) When psychologists are asked to provide services to individuals for whom appropriate mental health services are not available and for which psychologists have not obtained the competence necessary, psychologists with closely related prior training or experience may provide such services in order to ensure that services are not denied if they make a reasonable effort to obtain the competence required by using relevant research, training, consultation, or study.

(e) In those emerging areas in which generally recognized standards for preparatory training do not yet exist, psychologists nevertheless take reasonable steps to ensure the competence of their work and to protect clients/patients, students, supervisees, research participants, organizational clients, and others from harm.

(f) When assuming forensic roles, psychologists are or become reasonably familiar with the judicial or administrative rules governing their roles.

### 2.02 Providing Services in Emergencies

In emergencies, when psychologists provide services to individuals for whom other mental health services are not available and for which psychologists have not obtained the necessary training, psychologists may provide such services in order to ensure that services are not denied. The services are discontinued as soon as the emergency has ended or appropriate services are available.

### 2.03 Maintaining Competence

Psychologists undertake ongoing efforts to develop and maintain their competence.

### 2.04 Bases for Scientific and Professional Judgments

Psychologists' work is based upon established scientific and professional knowledge of the discipline. (See also Standards 2.01e, Boundaries of Competence, and 10.01b, Informed Consent to Therapy.)

### 2.05 Delegation of Work to Others

Psychologists who delegate work to employees, supervisees, or research or teaching assistants or who use the services of others, such as interpreters, take reasonable steps to (1) avoid delegating such work to persons who have a multiple relationship with those being served that would likely lead to exploitation or loss of objectivity; (2) authorize only those responsibilities that such persons can be expected to perform competently on the basis of their education, training, or experience, either independently or with the level of supervision being provided; and (3) see that such persons perform these services competently. (See also Standards 2.02, Providing Services in Emergencies; 3.05, Multiple Relationships; 4.01, Maintaining Confidentiality; 9.01, Bases for Assessments; 9.02, Use of Assessments; 9.03, Informed Consent in Assessments; and 9.07, Assessment by Unqualified Persons.)

### 2.06 Personal Problems and Conflicts

(a) Psychologists refrain from initiating an activity when they know or should know that there is a substantial likelihood that their personal problems will prevent them from performing their work-related activities in a competent manner.

(b) When psychologists become aware of personal problems that may interfere with their performing work-related duties adequately, they take appropriate measures, such as obtaining professional consultation or assistance, and determine whether they should limit, suspend, or terminate their work-related duties. (See also Standard 10.10, Terminating Therapy.)

### 3.  Human Relations

### 3.01 Unfair Discrimination

In their work-related activities, psychologists do not engage in unfair discrimination based on age, gender, gender identity, race, ethnicity, culture, national origin, religion, sexual orientation, disability, socioeconomic status, or any basis proscribed by law.

### 3.02 Sexual Harassment

Psychologists do not engage in sexual harassment. Sexual harassment is sexual solicitation, physical advances, or verbal or nonverbal conduct that is sexual in nature, that occurs in connection with the psychologist's activities or roles as a psychologist, and that either (1) is unwelcome, is offensive, or creates a hostile workplace or educational environment, and the psychologist knows or is told this or (2) is sufficiently severe or intense to be abusive to a reasonable person in the context. Sexual harassment can consist of a single intense or severe act or of multiple persistent or pervasive acts. (See also Standard 1.08, Unfair Discrimination Against Complainants and Respondents.)

### 3.03 Other Harassment

Psychologists do not knowingly engage in behavior that is harassing or demeaning to persons with whom they interact in their work based on factors such as those persons' age, gender, gender identity, race, ethnicity, culture, national origin, religion, sexual orientation, disability, language, or socioeconomic status.

### 3.04 Avoiding Harm

Psychologists take reasonable steps to avoid harming their clients/patients, students, supervisees, research participants, organizational clients, and others with whom they work, and to minimize harm where it is foreseeable and unavoidable.

### 3.05 Multiple Relationships

(a) A multiple relationship occurs when a psychologist is in a professional role with a person and (1) at the same time is in another role with the same person, (2) at the same time is in a relationship with a person closely associated with or related to the person with whom the psychologist has the professional relationship, or (3) promises to enter into another relationship in the future with the person or a person closely associated with or related to the person.

A psychologist refrains from entering into a multiple relationship if the multiple relationship could reasonably be expected to impair the psychologist's objectivity, competence, or effectiveness in performing his or her functions as a psychologist, or otherwise risks exploitation or harm to the person with whom the professional relationship exists.

Multiple relationships that would not reasonably be expected to cause impairment or risk exploitation or harm are not unethical.

(b) If a psychologist finds that, due to unforeseen factors, a potentially harmful multiple relationship has arisen, the psychologist takes reasonable steps to resolve it with due regard for the best interests of the affected person and maximal compliance with the Ethics Code

(c) When psychologists are required by law, institutional policy, or extraordinary circumstances to serve in more than one role in judicial or administrative proceedings, at the outset they clarify role expectations and the extent of confidentiality and thereafter as changes occur. (See also Standards 3.04, Avoiding Harm, and 3.07, Third-Party Requests for Services.)

### 3.06 Conflict of Interest

Psychologists refrain from taking on a professional role when personal, scientific, professional, legal, financial, or other interests or relationships could reasonably be expected to (1) impair their objectivity, competence, or effectiveness in performing their functions as psychologists or (2) expose the person or organization with whom the professional relationship exists to harm or exploitation.

### 3.07 Third-Party Requests for Services

When psychologists agree to provide services to a person or entity at the request of a third party, psychologists attempt to clarify at the outset of the service the nature of the relationship with all individuals or organizations involved. This clarification includes the role of the psychologist (e.g., therapist, consultant, diagnostician, or expert witness), an identification of who is the client, the probable uses of the services provided or the information obtained, and the fact that there may be limits to confidentiality. (See also Standards 3.05, Multiple Relationships, and 4.02, Discussing the Limits of Confidentiality.)

### 3.08 Exploitative Relationships
Psychologists do not exploit persons over whom they have supervisory, evaluative, or other authority such as clients/patients, students, supervisees, research participants, and employees. (See also Standards 3.05, Multiple Relationships; 6.04, Fees and Financial Arrangements; 6.05, Barter With Clients/Patients; 7.07, Sexual Relationships With Students and Supervisees; 10.05, Sexual Intimacies With Current Therapy Clients/Patients; 10.06, Sexual Intimacies With Relatives or Significant Others of Current Therapy Clients/Patients; 10.07, Therapy With Former Sexual Partners; and 10.08, Sexual Intimacies With Former Therapy Clients/Patients.)

### 3.09 Cooperation with Other Professionals
When indicated and professionally appropriate, psychologists cooperate with other professionals in order to serve their clients/patients effectively and appropriately. (See also Standard 4.05, Disclosures.)

### 3.10 Informed Consent
(a) When psychologists conduct research or provide assessment, therapy, counseling, or consulting services in person or via electronic transmission or other forms of communication, they obtain the informed consent of the individual or individuals using language that is reasonably understandable to that person or persons except when conducting such activities without consent is mandated by law or governmental regulation or as otherwise provided in this Ethics Code. (See also Standards 8.02, Informed Consent to Research; 9.03, Informed Consent in Assessments; and 10.01, Informed Consent to Therapy.)

(b) For persons who are legally incapable of giving informed consent, psychologists nevertheless (1) provide an appropriate explanation, (2) seek the individual's assent, (3) consider such persons' preferences and best interests, and (4) obtain appropriate permission from a legally authorized person, if such substitute consent is permitted or required by law. When consent by a legally authorized person is not permitted or required by law, psychologists take reasonable steps to protect the individual's rights and welfare.

(c) When psychological services are court ordered or otherwise mandated, psychologists inform the individual of the nature of the anticipated services, including whether the services are court ordered or mandated and any limits of confidentiality, before proceeding.

(d) Psychologists appropriately document written or oral consent, permission, and assent. (See also Standards 8.02, Informed Consent to Research; 9.03, Informed Consent in Assessments; and 10.01, Informed Consent to Therapy.)

### 3.11 Psychological Services Delivered to or Through Organizations
(a) Psychologists delivering services to or through organizations provide information beforehand to clients and when appropriate those directly affected by the services about (1) the nature and objectives of the services, (2) the intended recipients, (3) which of the individuals

are clients, (4) the relationship the psychologist will have with each person and the organization, (5) the probable uses of services provided and information obtained, (6) who will have access to the information, and (7) limits of confidentiality. As soon as feasible, they provide information about the results and conclusions of such services to appropriate persons.

(b) If psychologists will be precluded by law or by organizational roles from providing such information to particular individuals or groups, they so inform those individuals or groups at the outset of the service.

### 3.12 Interruption of Psychological Services

Unless otherwise covered by contract, psychologists make reasonable efforts to plan for facilitating services in the event that psychological services are interrupted by factors such as the psychologist's illness, death, unavailability, relocation, or retirement or by the client's/patient's relocation or financial limitations. (See also Standard 6.02c, Maintenance, Dissemination, and Disposal of Confidential Records of Professional and Scientific Work.)

## 4. Privacy and Confidentiality

### 4.01 Maintaining Confidentiality

Psychologists have a primary obligation and take reasonable precautions to protect confidential information obtained through or stored in any medium, recognizing that the extent and limits of confidentiality may be regulated by law or established by institutional rules or professional or scientific relationship. (See also Standard 2.05, Delegation of Work to Others.)

### 4.02 Discussing the Limits of Confidentiality

(a) Psychologists discuss with persons (including, to the extent feasible, persons who are legally incapable of giving informed consent and their legal representatives) and organizations with whom they establish a scientific or professional relationship (1) the relevant limits of confidentiality and (2) the foreseeable uses of the information generated through their psychological activities. (See also Standard 3.10, Informed Consent.)

(b) Unless it is not feasible or is contraindicated, the discussion of confidentiality occurs at the outset of the relationship and thereafter as new circumstances may warrant.

(c) Psychologists who offer services, products, or information via electronic transmission inform clients/patients of the risks to privacy and limits of confidentiality.

### 4.03 Recording

Before recording the voices or images of individuals to whom they provide services, psychologists obtain permission from all such persons or their legal representatives. (See also Standards 8.03, Informed Consent for Recording Voices and Images in Research; 8.05, Dispensing With Informed Consent for Research; and 8.07, Deception in Research.)

### 4.04 Minimizing Intrusions on Privacy

(a) Psychologists include in written and oral reports and consultations, only information germane to the purpose for which the communication is made.

(b) Psychologists discuss confidential information obtained in their work only for appropriate scientific or professional purposes and only with persons clearly concerned with such matters.

### 4.05 Disclosures

(a) Psychologists may disclose confidential information with the appropriate consent of the organizational client, the individual client/patient, or another legally authorized person on behalf of the client/patient unless prohibited by law.

(b) Psychologists disclose confidential information without the consent of the individual only as mandated by law, or where permitted by law for a valid purpose such as to (1) provide needed professional services; (2) obtain appropriate professional consultations; (3) protect the client/patient, psychologist, or others from harm; or (4) obtain payment for services from a client/patient, in which instance disclosure is limited to the minimum that is necessary to achieve the purpose. (See also Standard 6.04e, Fees and Financial Arrangements.)

### 4.06 Consultations

When consulting with colleagues, (1) psychologists do not disclose confidential information that reasonably could lead to the identification of a client/patient, research participant, or other person or organization with whom they have a confidential relationship unless they have obtained the prior consent of the person or organization or the disclosure cannot be avoided, and (2) they disclose information only to the extent necessary to achieve the purposes of the consultation. (See also Standard 4.01, Maintaining Confidentiality.)

### 4.07 Use of Confidential Information for Didactic or Other Purposes

Psychologists do not disclose in their writings, lectures, or other public media, confidential, personally identifiable information concerning their clients/patients, students, research participants, organizational clients, or other recipients of their services that they obtained during the course of their work, unless (1) they take reasonable steps to disguise the person or organization, (2) the person or organization has consented in writing, or (3) there is legal authorization for doing so.

### 5.  Advertising and Other Public Statements

### 5.01 Avoidance of False or Deceptive Statements

(a) Public statements include but are not limited to paid or unpaid advertising, product endorsements, grant applications, licensing applications, other credentialing applications, brochures, printed matter, directory listings, personal resumes or curricula vitae, or comments for use in media such as print or electronic transmission, statements in legal proceedings, lectures and public oral presentations, and published materials. Psychologists do not knowingly make public statements that are false, deceptive, or fraudulent concerning their research, practice, or other work activities or those of persons or organizations with which they are affiliated.

(b) Psychologists do not make false, deceptive, or fraudulent statements concerning (1) their training, experience, or competence; (2) their academic degrees; (3) their credentials; (4) their institutional or association affiliations; (5) their services; (6) the scientific or clinical basis for, or results or degree of success of, their services; (7) their fees; or (8) their publications or research findings.

(c) Psychologists claim degrees as credentials for their health services only if those degrees (1) were earned from a regionally accredited educational institution or (2) were the basis for psychology licensure by the state in which they practice.

## 5.02 Statements by Others

(a) Psychologists who engage others to create or place public statements that promote their professional practice, products, or activities retain professional responsibility for such statements.

(b) Psychologists do not compensate employees of press, radio, television, or other communication media in return for publicity in a news item. (See also Standard 1.01, Misuse of Psychologists' Work.)

(c) A paid advertisement relating to psychologists' activities must be identified or clearly recognizable as such.

## 5.03 Descriptions of Workshops and Non-Degree-Granting Educational Programs

To the degree to which they exercise control, psychologists responsible for announcements, catalogs, brochures, or advertisements describing workshops, seminars, or other non-degree-granting educational programs ensure that they accurately describe the audience for which the program is intended, the educational objectives, the presenters, and the fees involved.

## 5.04 Media Presentations

When psychologists provide public advice or comment via print, internet, or other electronic transmission, they take precautions to ensure that statements (1) are based on their professional knowledge, training, or experience in accord with appropriate psychological literature and practice; (2) are otherwise consistent with this Ethics Code; and (3) do not indicate that a professional relationship has been established with the recipient. (See also Standard 2.04, Bases for Scientific and Professional Judgments.)

## 5.05 Testimonials

Psychologists do not solicit testimonials from current therapy clients/patients or other persons who because of their particular circumstances are vulnerable to undue influence.

## 5.06 In-Person Solicitation

Psychologists do not engage, directly or through agents, in uninvited in-person solicitation of business from actual or potential therapy clients/patients or other persons who because of their particular circumstances are vulnerable to undue influence. However, this prohibition does not preclude (1) attempting to implement appropriate collateral contacts for the purpose of benefiting an already engaged therapy client/patient or (2) providing disaster or community outreach services.

## 6.   Record Keeping and Fees

## 6.01 Documentation of Professional and Scientific Work and Maintenance of Records

Psychologists create, and to the extent the records are under their control, maintain, disseminate, store, retain, and dispose of records and data relating to their professional and scientific work in order to (1) facilitate provision of services later by them or by other professionals, (2) allow for replication of research design and analyses, (3) meet institutional requirements, (4) ensure accuracy of billing and payments, and (5) ensure compliance with law. (See also Standard 4.01, Maintaining Confidentiality.)

### 6.02 Maintenance, Dissemination, and Disposal of Confidential Records of Professional and Scientific Work

(a) Psychologists maintain confidentiality in creating, storing, accessing, transferring, and disposing of records under their control, whether these are written, automated, or in any other medium. (See also Standards 4.01, Maintaining Confidentiality, and 6.01, Documentation of Professional and Scientific Work and Maintenance of Records.)

(b) If confidential information concerning recipients of psychological services is entered into databases or systems of records available to persons whose access has not been consented to by the recipient, psychologists use coding or other techniques to avoid the inclusion of personal identifiers.

(c) Psychologists make plans in advance to facilitate the appropriate transfer and to protect the confidentiality of records and data in the event of psychologists' withdrawal from positions or practice. (See also Standards 3.12, Interruption of Psychological Services, and 10.09, Interruption of Therapy.)

### 6.03 Withholding Records for Nonpayment

Psychologists may not withhold records under their control that are requested and needed for a client's/patient's emergency treatment solely because payment has not been received.

### 6.04 Fees and Financial Arrangements

(a) As early as is feasible in a professional or scientific relationship, psychologists and recipients of psychological services reach an agreement specifying compensation and billing arrangements.

(b) Psychologists' fee practices are consistent with law.

(c) Psychologists do not misrepresent their fees.

(d) If limitations to services can be anticipated because of limitations in financing, this is discussed with the recipient of services as early as is feasible. (See also Standards 10.09, Interruption of Therapy, and 10.10, Terminating Therapy.)

(e) If the recipient of services does not pay for services as agreed, and if psychologists intend to use collection agencies or legal measures to collect the fees, psychologists first inform the person that such measures will be taken and provide that person an opportunity to make prompt payment. (See also Standards 4.05, Disclosures; 6.03, Withholding Records for Nonpayment; and 10.01, Informed Consent to Therapy.)

### 6.05 Barter with Clients/Patients

Barter is the acceptance of goods, services, or other nonmonetary remuneration from clients/patients in return for psychological services. Psychologists may barter only if (1) it is not clinically contraindicated, and (2) the resulting arrangement is not exploitative. (See also Standards 3.05, Multiple Relationships, and 6.04, Fees and Financial Arrangements.)

### 6.06 Accuracy in Reports to Payors and Funding Sources

In their reports to payors for services or sources of research funding, psychologists take reasonable steps to ensure the accurate reporting of the nature of the service provided or research conducted, the fees, charges, or payments, and where applicable, the identity of the provider, the findings, and the diagnosis. (See also Standards 4.01, Maintaining Confidentiality; 4.04, Minimizing Intrusions on Privacy; and 4.05, Disclosures.)

## 6.07 Referrals and Fees

When psychologists pay, receive payment from, or divide fees with another professional, other than in an employer-employee relationship, the payment to each is based on the services provided (clinical, consultative, administrative, or other) and is not based on the referral itself. (See also Standard 3.09, Cooperation With Other Professionals.)

## 7. Education and Training

### 7.01 Design of Education and Training Programs

Psychologists responsible for education and training programs take reasonable steps to ensure that the programs are designed to provide the appropriate knowledge and proper experiences, and to meet the requirements for licensure, certification, or other goals for which claims are made by the program. (See also Standard 5.03, Descriptions of Workshops and Non-Degree-Granting Educational Programs.)

### 7.02 Descriptions of Education and Training Programs

Psychologists responsible for education and training programs take reasonable steps to ensure that there is a current and accurate description of the program content (including participation in required course- or program-related counseling, psychotherapy, experiential groups, consulting projects, or community service), training goals and objectives, stipends and benefits, and requirements that must be met for satisfactory completion of the program. This information must be made readily available to all interested parties.

### 7.03 Accuracy in Teaching

(a) Psychologists take reasonable steps to ensure that course syllabi are accurate regarding the subject matter to be covered, bases for evaluating progress, and the nature of course experiences. This standard does not preclude an instructor from modifying course content or requirements when the instructor considers it pedagogically necessary or desirable, so long as students are made aware of these modifications in a manner that enables them to fulfill course requirements. (See also Standard 5.01, Avoidance of False or Deceptive Statements.)

(b) When engaged in teaching or training, psychologists present psychological information accurately. (See also Standard 2.03, Maintaining Competence.)

### 7.04 Student Disclosure of Personal Information

Psychologists do not require students or supervisees to disclose personal information in course- or program-related activities, either orally or in writing, regarding sexual history, history of abuse and neglect, psychological treatment, and relationships with parents, peers, and spouses or significant others except if (1) the program or training facility has clearly identified this requirement in its admissions and program materials or (2) the information is necessary to evaluate or obtain assistance for students whose personal problems could reasonably be judged to be preventing them from performing their training- or professionally related activities in a competent manner or posing a threat to the students or others.

### 7.05 Mandatory Individual or Group Therapy

(a) When individual or group therapy is a program or course requirement, psychologists responsible for that program allow students in undergraduate and graduate programs the option of selecting such therapy from practitioners unaffiliated with the program. (See also Standard 7.02, Descriptions of Education and Training Programs.)

(b) Faculty who are or are likely to be responsible for evaluating students' academic performance do not themselves provide that therapy. (See also Standard 3.05, Multiple Relationships.)

### 7.06 Assessing Student and Supervisee Performance

(a) In academic and supervisory relationships, psychologists establish a timely and specific process for providing feedback to students and supervisees. Information regarding the process is provided to the student at the beginning of supervision.

(b) Psychologists evaluate students and supervisees on the basis of their actual performance on relevant and established program requirements.

### 7.07 Sexual Relationships with Students and Supervisees

Psychologists do not engage in sexual relationships with students or supervisees who are in their department, agency, or training center or over whom psychologists have or are likely to have evaluative authority. (See also Standard 3.05, Multiple Relationships.)

### 8.   Research and Publication

### 8.01 Institutional Approval

When institutional approval is required, psychologists provide accurate information about their research proposals and obtain approval prior to conducting the research. They conduct the research in accordance with the approved research protocol.

### 8.02 Informed Consent to Research

(a) When obtaining informed consent as required in Standard 3.10, Informed Consent, psychologists inform participants about (1) the purpose of the research, expected duration, and procedures; (2) their right to decline to participate and to withdraw from the research once participation has begun; (3) the foreseeable consequences of declining or withdrawing; (4) reasonably foreseeable factors that may be expected to influence their willingness to participate such as potential risks, discomfort, or adverse effects; (5) any prospective research benefits; (6) limits of confidentiality; (7) incentives for participation; and (8) whom to contact for questions about the research and research participants' rights. They provide opportunity for the prospective participants to ask questions and receive answers. (See also Standards 8.03, Informed Consent for Recording Voices and Images in Research; 8.05, Dispensing With Informed Consent for Research; and 8.07, Deception in Research.)

(b) Psychologists conducting intervention research involving the use of experimental treatments clarify to participants at the outset of the research (1) the experimental nature of the treatment; (2) the services that will or will not be available to the control group(s) if appropriate; (3) the means by which assignment to treatment and control groups will be made;

(4) available treatment alternatives if an individual does not wish to participate in the research or wishes to withdraw once a study has begun; and (5) compensation for or monetary costs of participating including, if appropriate, whether reimbursement from the participant or a third-party payor will be sought. (See also Standard 8.02a, Informed Consent to Research.)

### 8.03 Informed Consent for Recording Voices and Images in Research

Psychologists obtain informed consent from research participants prior to recording their voices or images for data collection unless (1) the research consists solely of naturalistic observations in public places, and it is not anticipated that the recording will be used in a manner that could cause personal identification or harm, or (2) the research design includes deception, and consent for the use of the recording is obtained during debriefing. (See also Standard 8.07, Deception in Research.)

### 8.04 Client/Patient, Student, and Subordinate Research Participants

(a) When psychologists conduct research with clients/patients, students, or subordinates as participants, psychologists take steps to protect the prospective participants from adverse consequences of declining or withdrawing from participation.

(b) When research participation is a course requirement or an opportunity for extra credit, the prospective participant is given the choice of equitable alternative activities.

### 8.05 Dispensing with Informed Consent for Research

Psychologists may dispense with informed consent only (1) where research would not reasonably be assumed to create distress or harm and involves (a) the study of normal educational practices, curricula, or classroom management methods conducted in educational settings; (b) only anonymous questionnaires, naturalistic observations, or archival research for which disclosure of responses would not place participants at risk of criminal or civil liability or damage their financial standing, employability, or reputation, and confidentiality is protected; or (c) the study of factors related to job or organization effectiveness conducted in organizational settings for which there is no risk to participants' employability, and confidentiality is protected or (2) where otherwise permitted by law or federal or institutional regulations.

### 8.06 Offering Inducements for Research Participation

(a) Psychologists make reasonable efforts to avoid offering excessive or inappropriate financial or other inducements for research participation when such inducements are likely to coerce participation.

(b) When offering professional services as an inducement for research participation, psychologists clarify the nature of the services, as well as the risks, obligations, and limitations. (See also Standard 6.05, Barter With Clients/Patients.)

### 8.07 Deception in Research

(a) Psychologists do not conduct a study involving deception unless they have determined that the use of deceptive techniques is justified by the study's significant prospective scientific, educational, or applied value and that effective nondeceptive alternative procedures are not feasible.

(b) Psychologists do not deceive prospective participants about research that is reasonably expected to cause physical pain or severe emotional distress.

(c) Psychologists explain any deception that is an integral feature of the design and conduct of an experiment to participants as early as is feasible, preferably at the conclusion of their participation, but no later than at the conclusion of the data collection, and permit participants to withdraw their data. (See also Standard 8.08, Debriefing.)

### 8.08 Debriefing

(a) Psychologists provide a prompt opportunity for participants to obtain appropriate information about the nature, results, and conclusions of the research, and they take reasonable steps to correct any misconceptions that participants may have of which the psychologists are aware.

(b) If scientific or humane values justify delaying or withholding this information, psychologists take reasonable measures to reduce the risk of harm.

(c) When psychologists become aware that research procedures have harmed a participant, they take reasonable steps to minimize the harm.

### 8.09 Humane Care and Use of Animals in Research

(a) Psychologists acquire, care for, use, and dispose of animals in compliance with current federal, state, and local laws and regulations, and with professional standards.

(b) Psychologists trained in research methods and experienced in the care of laboratory animals supervise all procedures involving animals and are responsible for ensuring appropriate consideration of their comfort, health, and humane treatment.

(c) Psychologists ensure that all individuals under their supervision who are using animals have received instruction in research methods and in the care, maintenance, and handling of the species being used, to the extent appropriate to their role. (See also Standard 2.05, Delegation of Work to Others.)

(d) Psychologists make reasonable efforts to minimize the discomfort, infection, illness, and pain of animal subjects.

(e) Psychologists use a procedure subjecting animals to pain, stress, or privation only when an alternative procedure is unavailable and the goal is justified by its prospective scientific, educational, or applied value.

(f) Psychologists perform surgical procedures under appropriate anesthesia and follow techniques to avoid infection and minimize pain during and after surgery.

(g) When it is appropriate that an animal's life be terminated, psychologists proceed rapidly, with an effort to minimize pain and in accordance with accepted procedures.

### 8.10 Reporting Research Results

(a) Psychologists do not fabricate data. (See also Standard 5.01a, Avoidance of False or Deceptive Statements.)

(b) If psychologists discover significant errors in their published data, they take reasonable steps to correct such errors in a correction, retraction, erratum, or other appropriate publication means.

### 8.11 Plagiarism

Psychologists do not present portions of another's work or data as their own, even if the other work or data source is cited occasionally.

### 8.12 Publication Credit

(a) Psychologists take responsibility and credit, including authorship credit, only for work they have actually performed or to which they have substantially contributed. (See also Standard 8.12b, Publication Credit.)

(b) Principal authorship and other publication credits accurately reflect the relative scientific or professional contributions of the individuals involved, regardless of their relative status. Mere possession of an institutional position, such as department chair, does not justify authorship credit. Minor contributions to the research or to the writing for publications are acknowledged appropriately, such as in footnotes or in an introductory statement.

(c) Except under exceptional circumstances, a student is listed as principal author on any multiple-authored article that is substantially based on the student's doctoral dissertation. Faculty advisors discuss publication credit with students as early as feasible and throughout the research and publication process as appropriate. (See also Standard 8.12b, Publication Credit.)

### 8.13 Duplicate Publication of Data

Psychologists do not publish, as original data, data that have been previously published. This does not preclude republishing data when they are accompanied by proper acknowledgment.

### 8.14 Sharing Research Data for Verification

(a) After research results are published, psychologists do not withhold the data on which their conclusions are based from other competent professionals who seek to verify the substantive claims through reanalysis and who intend to use such data only for that purpose, provided that the confidentiality of the participants can be protected and unless legal rights concerning proprietary data preclude their release. This does not preclude psychologists from requiring that such individuals or groups be responsible for costs associated with the provision of such information.

(b) Psychologists who request data from other psychologists to verify the substantive claims through reanalysis may use shared data only for the declared purpose. Requesting psychologists obtain prior written agreement for all other uses of the data.

### 8.15 Reviewers

Psychologists who review material submitted for presentation, publication, grant, or research proposal review respect the confidentiality of and the proprietary rights in such information of those who submitted it.

### 9. Assessment

### 9.01 Bases for Assessments

(a) Psychologists base the opinions contained in their recommendations, reports, and diagnostic or evaluative statements, including forensic testimony, on information and techniques sufficient to substantiate their findings. (See also Standard 2.04, Bases for Scientific and Professional Judgments.)

(b) Except as noted in 9.01c, psychologists provide opinions of the psychological characteristics of individuals only after they have conducted an examination of the individuals adequate to support their statements or conclusions. When, despite reasonable efforts, such an examination is not practical, psychologists document the efforts they made and the result of those efforts, clarify the probable impact of their limited information on the reliability and validity of their opinions, and appropriately limit the nature and extent of their conclusions or recommendations. (See also Standards 2.01, Boundaries of Competence, and 9.06, Interpreting Assessment Results.)

(c) When psychologists conduct a record review or provide consultation or supervision and an individual examination is not warranted or necessary for the opinion, psychologists explain this and the sources of information on which they based their conclusions and recommendations.

### 9.02 Use of Assessments

(a) Psychologists administer, adapt, score, interpret, or use assessment techniques, interviews, tests, or instruments in a manner and for purposes that are appropriate in light of the research on or evidence of the usefulness and proper application of the techniques.

(b) Psychologists use assessment instruments whose validity and reliability have been established for use with members of the population tested. When such validity or reliability has not been established, psychologists describe the strengths and limitations of test results and interpretation.

(c) Psychologists use assessment methods that are appropriate to an individual's language preference and competence, unless the use of an alternative language is relevant to the assessment issues.

### 9.03 Informed Consent in Assessments

(a) Psychologists obtain informed consent for assessments, evaluations, or diagnostic services, as described in Standard 3.10, Informed Consent, except when (1) testing is mandated by law or governmental regulations; (2) informed consent is implied because testing is conducted as a routine educational, institutional, or organizational activity (e.g., when participants voluntarily agree to assessment when applying for a job); or (3) one purpose of the testing is to evaluate decisional capacity. Informed consent includes an explanation of the nature and purpose of the assessment, fees, involvement of third parties, and limits of confidentiality and sufficient opportunity for the client/patient to ask questions and receive answers.

(b) Psychologists inform persons with questionable capacity to consent or for whom testing is mandated by law or governmental regulations about the nature and purpose of the proposed assessment services, using language that is reasonably understandable to the person being assessed.

(c) Psychologists using the services of an interpreter obtain informed consent from the client/patient to use that interpreter, ensure that confidentiality of test results and test security are maintained, and include in their recommendations, reports, and diagnostic or evaluative statements, including forensic testimony, discussion of any limitations on the data obtained. (See also Standards 2.05, Delegation of Work to Others; 4.01, Maintaining Confidentiality; 9.01, Bases for Assessments; 9.06, Interpreting Assessment Results; and 9.07, Assessment by Unqualified Persons.)

## 9.04 Release of Test Data

(a) The term *test data* refers to raw and scaled scores, client/patient responses to test questions or stimuli, and psychologists' notes and recordings concerning client/patient statements and behavior during an examination. Those portions of test materials that include client/patient responses are included in the definition of *test data*. Pursuant to a client/patient release, psychologists provide test data to the client/patient or other persons identified in the release. Psychologists may refrain from releasing test data to protect a client/patient or others from substantial harm or misuse or misrepresentation of the data or the test, recognizing that in many instances release of confidential information under these circumstances is regulated by law. (See also Standard 9.11, Maintaining Test Security.)

(b) In the absence of a client/patient release, psychologists provide test data only as required by law or court order.

## 9.05 Test Construction

Psychologists who develop tests and other assessment techniques use appropriate psychometric procedures and current scientific or professional knowledge for test design, standardization, validation, reduction or elimination of bias, and recommendations for use.

## 9.06 Interpreting Assessment Results

When interpreting assessment results, including automated interpretations, psychologists take into account the purpose of the assessment as well as the various test factors, test-taking abilities, and other characteristics of the person being assessed, such as situational, personal, linguistic, and cultural differences, that might affect psychologists' judgments or reduce the accuracy of their interpretations. They indicate any significant limitations of their interpretations. (See also Standards 2.01b and c, Boundaries of Competence, and 3.01, Unfair Discrimination.)

## 9.07 Assessment by Unqualified Persons

Psychologists do not promote the use of psychological assessment techniques by unqualified persons, except when such use is conducted for training purposes with appropriate supervision. (See also Standard 2.05, Delegation of Work to Others.)

## 9.08 Obsolete Tests and Outdated Test Results

(a) Psychologists do not base their assessment or intervention decisions or recommendations on data or test results that are outdated for the current purpose.

(b) Psychologists do not base such decisions or recommendations on tests and measures that are obsolete and not useful for the current purpose.

## 9.09 Test Scoring and Interpretation Services

(a) Psychologists who offer assessment or scoring services to other professionals accurately describe the purpose, norms, validity, reliability, and applications of the procedures and any special qualifications applicable to their use.

(b) Psychologists select scoring and interpretation services (including automated services) on the basis of evidence of the validity of the program and procedures as well as on other appropriate considerations. (See also Standard 2.01b and c, Boundaries of Competence.)

(c) Psychologists retain responsibility for the appropriate application, interpretation, and use of assessment instruments, whether they score and interpret such tests themselves or use automated or other services.

### 9.10 Explaining Assessment Results

Regardless of whether the scoring and interpretation are done by psychologists, by employees or assistants, or by automated or other outside services, psychologists take reasonable steps to ensure that explanations of results are given to the individual or designated representative unless the nature of the relationship precludes provision of an explanation of results (such as in some organizational consulting, preemployment or security screenings, and forensic evaluations), and this fact has been clearly explained to the person being assessed in advance.

### 9.11. Maintaining Test Security

The term *test materials* refers to manuals, instruments, protocols, and test questions or stimuli and does not include *test data* as defined in Standard 9.04, Release of Test Data. Psychologists make reasonable efforts to maintain the integrity and security of test materials and other assessment techniques consistent with law and contractual obligations, and in a manner that permits adherence to this Ethics Code.

### 10.  Therapy

### 10.01 Informed Consent to Therapy

(a) When obtaining informed consent to therapy as required in Standard 3.10, Informed Consent, psychologists inform clients/patients as early as is feasible in the therapeutic relationship about the nature and anticipated course of therapy, fees, involvement of third parties, and limits of confidentiality and provide sufficient opportunity for the client/patient to ask questions and receive answers. (See also Standards 4.02, Discussing the Limits of Confidentiality, and 6.04, Fees and Financial Arrangements.)

(b) When obtaining informed consent for treatment for which generally recognized techniques and procedures have not been established, psychologists inform their clients/patients of the developing nature of the treatment, the potential risks involved, alternative treatments that may be available, and the voluntary nature of their participation. (See also Standards 2.01e, Boundaries of Competence, and 3.10, Informed Consent.)

(c) When the therapist is a trainee and the legal responsibility for the treatment provided resides with the supervisor, the client/patient, as part of the informed consent procedure, is informed that the therapist is in training and is being supervised and is given the name of the supervisor.

### 10.02 Therapy Involving Couples or Families

(a) When psychologists agree to provide services to several persons who have a relationship (such as spouses, significant others, or parents and children), they take reasonable steps to clarify at the outset (1) which of the individuals are clients/patients and (2) the relationship the psychologist will have with each person. This clarification includes the psychologist's role and the probable uses of the services provided or the information obtained. (See also Standard 4.02, Discussing the Limits of Confidentiality.)

(b) If it becomes apparent that psychologists may be called on to perform potentially conflicting roles (such as family therapist and then witness for one party in divorce proceedings), psychologists take reasonable steps to clarify and modify, or withdraw from, roles appropriately. (See also Standard 3.05c, Multiple Relationships.)

## 10.03 Group Therapy

When psychologists provide services to several persons in a group setting, they describe at the outset the roles and responsibilities of all parties and the limits of confidentiality.

## 10.04 Providing Therapy to Those Served by Others

In deciding whether to offer or provide services to those already receiving mental health services elsewhere, psychologists carefully consider the treatment issues and the potential client's/patient's welfare. Psychologists discuss these issues with the client/patient or another legally authorized person on behalf of the client/patient in order to minimize the risk of confusion and conflict, consult with the other service providers when appropriate, and proceed with caution and sensitivity to the therapeutic issues.

## 10.05 Sexual Intimacies with Current Therapy Clients/Patients

Psychologists do not engage in sexual intimacies with current therapy clients/patients.

## 10.06 Sexual Intimacies with Relatives or Significant Others of Current Therapy Clients/Patients

Psychologists do not engage in sexual intimacies with individuals they know to be close relatives, guardians, or significant others of current clients/patients. Psychologists do not terminate therapy to circumvent this standard.

## 10.07 Therapy with Former Sexual Partners

Psychologists do not accept as therapy clients/patients persons with whom they have engaged in sexual intimacies.

## 10.08 Sexual Intimacies with Former Therapy Clients/Patients

(a) Psychologists do not engage in sexual intimacies with former clients/patients for at least two years after cessation or termination of therapy.

(b) Psychologists do not engage in sexual intimacies with former clients/patients even after a two-year interval except in the most unusual circumstances. Psychologists who engage in such activity after the two years following cessation or termination of therapy and of having no sexual contact with the former client/patient bear the burden of demonstrating that there has been no exploitation, in light of all relevant factors, including (1) the amount of time that has passed since therapy terminated; (2) the nature, duration, and intensity of the therapy; (3) the circumstances of termination; (4) the client's/patient's personal history; (5) the client's/patient's current mental status; (6) the likelihood of adverse impact on the client/patient; and (7) any statements or actions made by the therapist during the course of therapy suggesting or inviting the possibility of a posttermination sexual or romantic relationship with the client/patient. (See also Standard 3.05, Multiple Relationships.)

### 10.09 Interruption of Therapy

When entering into employment or contractual relationships, psychologists make reasonable efforts to provide for orderly and appropriate resolution of responsibility for client/patient care in the event that the employment or contractual relationship ends, with paramount consideration given to the welfare of the client/patient. (See also Standard 3.12, Interruption of Psychological Services.)

### 10.10 Terminating Therapy

(a) Psychologists terminate therapy when it becomes reasonably clear that the client/patient no longer needs the service, is not likely to benefit, or is being harmed by continued service.

(b) Psychologists may terminate therapy when threatened or otherwise endangered by the client/patient or another person with whom the client/patient has a relationship.

(c) Except where precluded by the actions of clients/patients or third-party payors, prior to termination psychologists provide pretermination counseling and suggest alternative service providers as appropriate.

### History and Effective Date Footnote

This version of the APA Ethics Code was adopted by the American Psychological Association's Council of Representatives during its meeting, August 21, 2002, and is effective beginning June 1, 2003. Inquiries concerning the substance or interpretation of the APA Ethics Code should be addressed to the Director, Office of Ethics, American Psychological Association, 750 First Street, NE, Washington, DC 20002-4242. The Ethics Code and information regarding the Code can be found on the APA web site, http://www.apa.org/ethics. The standards in this Ethics Code will be used to adjudicate complaints brought concerning alleged conduct occurring on or after the effective date. Complaints regarding conduct occurring prior to the effective date will be adjudicated on the basis of the version of the Ethics Code that was in effect at the time the conduct occurred.

The APA has previously published its Ethics Code as follows:

American Psychological Association. (1953). Ethical standards of psychologists. Washington, DC: Author.

American Psychological Association. (1959). Ethical standards of psychologists. American Psychologist, 14, 279-282.

American Psychological Association. (1963). Ethical standards of psychologists. American Psychologist, 18, 56-60.

American Psychological Association. (1968). Ethical standards of psychologists. American Psychologist, 23, 357-361.

American Psychological Association. (1977, March). Ethical standards of psychologists. APA Monitor, 22-23.

American Psychological Association. (1979). Ethical standards of psychologists. Washington, DC: Author.

American Psychological Association. (1981). Ethical principles of psychologists. American Psychologist, 36, 633-638.

American Psychological Association. (1990). Ethical principles of psychologists (Amended June 2, 1989). American Psychologist, 45, 390-395.

American Psychological Association. (1992). Ethical principles of psychologists and code of conduct. American Psychologist, 47, 1597-1611.

Request copies of the APA's Ethical Principles of Psychologists and Code of Conduct from the APA Order Department, 750 First Street, NE, Washington, DC 20002-4242, or phone (202) 336-5510.

# A GUIDE FOR HARVARD STUDENTS: HOW TO AVOID HIGH-RISK SITUATIONS

Harvey, G. (1995). *Writing with sources: A guide for Harvard students. Expository writing program.* The President and Fellows of Harvard University. Retrieved from: http://www.fas.harvard.edu/~expos/sources/.

1. ***Don't leave written work until the last minute,*** when you may be surprised by how much work the assignment requires. This doesn't mean that you need to draft the paper weeks in advance (you can start working on a paper by simply jotting a few words or thoughts somewhere), but it does mean looking over the instructions for the assignment early on, jotting any first impressions, clearing up any confusions with your instructor, and getting the topic into your subsconscious mind, which can help you flag potentially useful material in subsequent reading and lectures. (If you feel you have a special fear or block about writing papers, or procrastinate excessively, or just don't seem to be able to organize and prioritize work, make an appointment at [The Learning Resource Center].)

2. ***Don't use secondary sources for a paper unless you are asked or explicitly allowed to.*** Especially, if you feel stuck or panicked, don't run to the library and bring back an armload of sources that you hope will jump-start your own thinking. Chances are they will only scatter and paralyze your thinking. Instead, go to your instructor . . . for advice or try jump-starting your paper in another way (e.g., by freewriting or brainstorming, by re-analyzing the assignment itself, by formulating a hard question for yourself to answer, by locating a problem or conflict, or by picking a few key passages and annotating them copiously).

3. ***Don't rely exclusively on a single secondary source for information or opinion*** in a research paper. If you do, your paper may be less well-informed and balanced that it should be, and moreover you may be lulled into plagiarizing the source. Using several different sources forces you to step back and evaluate or triangulate them.

4. ***When you take notes, take pains to distinguish the words and thoughts of the source from your own,*** so you don't mistake them for your own later. Adopt these habits in particular:

   - Either summarize radically or quote exactly, always using quotation marks when you quote. Don't take notes by loosely copying out source material and simply changing a few words.

   - When you take a note or quote from a source, jot the author's name and page number beside each note you take (don't simply jot down ideas anonymously), and record the source's publication data on that same page in your notes, to save yourself having to dig it up as you are rushing to finish your paper. Save even more time by recording this information in the same order and format you will use for listing references on your final draft.

- Take or transcribe your notes on sources in a separate word-processing file, not in the file in which you are drafting your paper. And keep these files separate throughout the writing of the paper, bringing in source material from your notes only as needed.

5. ***Take notes actively, not passively.*** Don't just copy down the source's words or ideas, but record your own reactions and reflections, questions, and hunches. Note where you find yourself resisting or doubting or puzzling over what a source says; jot down possible arguments or observations you might want to make. These will provide starting points when you turn to write your paper; and they will help keep you from feeling overwhelmed by your sources or your notes.

6. ***Don't try to sound more sophisticated or learned than you are.*** Your papers aren't expected to sound as erudite as the books and articles of your expert sources, and indeed your intelligence will emerge most clearly in a plain, direct style. Moreover, once you begin to appropriate a voice that isn't yours, it becomes easier accidentally to appropriate words and ideas to plagiarize. Also remember that, when asked to write a research paper using secondary sources, you are expected to learn from those sources but not to have the same level of knowledge and originality, or to resolve issues that experts have been debating for years. Your task is to clarify the issues and bring out their complexity. The way you organize the material to do this, if you take the task seriously, will be original.

7. ***If you feel stuck, confused, or panicked about time, or if you are having problems in your life and can't concentrate, let your instructor or section leader know.*** Make contact by e-mail, if it's easier for you, but do make contact, even if you feel embarrassed because you haven't attended lectures . . . or think you're the only student in the class who is having trouble (you aren't), or if you will have to lose points for a late paper. Losing points will be a much smaller event, in the story of your life, than . . . [failing] for plagiarism.

8. ***Don't ask to borrow another student's paper*** if you are stuck or running late with an assignment. Reading it will probably discourage or panic rather than inspire you, and it may tempt you to plagiarize. Instead, ask the student to help you brainstorm some of your own ideas.

9. ***Don't write a paper from borrowed notes,*** since you have no way of knowing the source or the words and ideas. They may, for example, come directly from a book or lecture, or from a book discussed in lecture.

10. ***Don't do the actual writing of a paper with another student,*** or split the writing between you, unless you have explicit permission. Even if you collaborate on a project, you're expected to express the results in your own words.

11. ***Don't submit to one class a paper or even sections of a paper, that you have submitted or will submit to another class,*** without first getting the written permission of both instructors. . . .

12. ***Always back up your work on diskette, and make a hard copy each time you end a long working session or finish a paper.*** This will reduce your chances of finding yourself in a desperate situation caused by computer failure.

# IF YOU ENCOUNTER "YOUR" IDEA IN A SOURCE

Don't pretend that you never encountered the source; but don't panic either. If it's your major idea and you're near the end of work on the paper, finish writing your argument as you have conceived it. Then look closely at the source in question: chances are that its idea isn't exactly the same as yours, that you have a slightly different emphasis or slant, or that you are considering somewhat different topics and evidence. In this case you can either mention and cite the source in the course of your argument (*"my contention, like Ann Harrison's, is that . . ."* or *"I share Ann Harrison's view that . . ."*), but stress the differences in your account, what you have noticed that Harrison hasn't. Or you can go back and recast your argument slightly, to make it distinct from the source's. If the argument in the source really is the same as yours, and you are in the midst of a long paper, go to your instructor, who may be able to suggest a slightly different direction for your paper. If you aren't writing a big paper, and haven't time to recast, use a note of acknowledgement:

12. In the final stages of writing this paper I discovered Ann Harrison's article "Echo and her Medieval Sisters," *Centennial Review* 26.4 (Fall 1982), 326–340, which comes to the same conclusion. See pp. 331–2.

Don't try to use such a note to cover plagiarism. Your instructor will know from your paper whether you had your own, well-developed ideas before reading the source, and may ask you to produce your rough notes or drafts. (To be safe, always hold on to your notes and drafts until a paper has been returned.)

# BIBLIOGRAPHY

Astin, A. W., & Astin, H. S. (2003). *Spirituality in college students: Preliminary findings from a national study.* Higher Education Research Institute, Los Angeles: UCLA, 1–6.

Barone, D. (1990). The written responses of young children: Beyond comprehension to story understanding. *The New Advocate,* 3, 49–56.

Beers, K. (2003). *When kids can't read: What teachers can do.* Portsmouth, NH: Heinemann.

Bennett, W. J. (1993). *The book of virtues: A treasury of great moral stories.* New York: Simon & Schuster.

Berthoff, A. E. (1981). *The making of meaning.* Montclair, NJ: Boynton/Cook.

Bilger, Burkhard. (2004). The Height Gap. *New Yorker,* April 5, 38–45.

Billing, S. H. (2000). The effects of service learning. *The School Administrator Web Edition.* Retrieved from: www.aasa.org/publicatins/sa/2000_08/billig.htm.

Biography. (1998). *Charles Darwin: Evolution's voice.* (Motion picture) New York.

Botstein, L. (1997). *Jefferson's Children: Education and the promise of American culture.* New York: Doubleday Dell Pub.

Bruner, J. S. (1966). *Toward a theory of instruction.* Cambridge, MA: Harvard University Press: In Entwistle, N. (1988). *Styles of learning and teaching, an integrated outline of educational psychology.* London: David Fulton Pubs.

Bruner, J. S. (1960). *The process of education.* Cambridge, MA: Harvard University Press.

Burns, Diane. (2002). Sure you can ask me a personal question. *The Bedford Introduction to Literature,* 6th ed. (Ed. Michael Meyer). Boston: Bedford/St. Martin's.

Chickering, A., & Ehrmann, S. C. (1996). *Implementing the Seven Principles: Technology as Lever.* Retrieved from: *AAHE Bulletin,* October, 3–6.

Chickering, A. W., Gamson, Z. F. (1987). Principles for good practice in undergraduate education. *The Wingspread Journal: Special Section.* Racine, WI: The Johnson Foundation.

Chittister, J. D., O.S.B. (1992). *The Rule of Benedict: Insights for the ages.* New York: The Crossroad Publishing Co.

Chittister, J. D., O.S.B. (1991). *Wisdom distilled from the daily: Living the Rule of St. Benedict today.* New York: Harper Collins Publishers.

Clinton, H. R. (1996). *It takes a village.* New York: Simon & Schuster.

Colby, A. (2000). *Whose values anyway?* Address presented at the 2000 Institute on College Values. Retrieved from: www.college.values.org.

Coles, R. (1990). *The spiritual life of children.* Boston: Houghton Mifflin.

Coles, R. Genevie, L. (1990). The moral life of America's school children. *Teacher Magazine,* 3.

Corcodilos, N. A. (1997). *Ask the headhunter: Reinventing the interview to write the job.* New York: Penguin Books.

Crain, W. C. (1985). *Theories of development.* Prentice Hall. Retrieved from http://faculty.plts.edu/gpence/html/kohlberg.htm.

Damon, W. (Ed.). (2002). *Bringing in a new era in character education.* Stanford, CA: Hoover Institution Press.

Davis, L. E., & Proctor, E. K. (1995). *Race, gender, and class: Guidelines for practice with individuals, families, and groups.* Englewood Cliffs, NJ: Prentice-Hall.

Delattre, E. (1990). Teaching integrity: The boundaries of moral education. *Education Week,* 9, 5, Commentary.

DeNicola, D. (1986). Liberal arts and business. *Nation's Business,* 4.

DeVries, R., & Zan, B. (1994). *Moral classrooms, moral children: Creating a constructivist atmosphere in early education.* New York: Teachers College Press.

Ditchazy, H. E. R., & Tiao, N. C. (2003). Returning to an emphasis on values and spirituality. *Delta Kappa Gamma Bulletin,* 69(3), 15–20.

Dobrin, A. (2001). Finding universal values in a time of relativism. *The Educational Forum,* 65(3), 273–278.

Doyle, L. J. (1948). *Saint Benedict's Rule for monasteries.* Collegeville, MN: The Liturgical Press.

*Dr. Fatkins Resolutionary Diet: How to eat what you want and pretend to lose weight.* (2004). London: Carlton.

Elder, L., & Paul, R. (2003). *A miniature guide for students and faculty to the foundations of analytic thinking: How to take thinking apart and what to look for when you do: The elements of thinking and the standards they must meet.* Dillon Beach, CA: Foundation for Critical Thinking.

Etzioni, A. (1994). U.S. schools rediscover the virtue of virtues. *Insight,* 12, 26.

Fields-Meyer, T., Birbeck, M., Kapos, S., Swertlow, F., & Spellman, C. R. (2004, March 1). Pirates of the Internet. *People Magazine,* 61, 8.

Frieden, G., & Pawelski, J. (2003). Affected development in college students: Strategies that promote ethical decision-making. *Journal of College Character,* 2. Retrieved from: www.collegevalues.org.

Fry, T., O.S.B. (Ed.). (1982). *RB 1980: The Rule of Saint Benedict in English,* Collegeville, MN: The Liturgical Press.

Gardner, J. N., & Jewler, A. J. (2004). *Your college experience: Strategies for success.* (5th ed.) Wadsworth Group, Thomson Learning Inc.

Goodman, J. F., & Lesnick, H. (2004). *Moral education: A teacher-centered approach.* Boston: Pearson Education, Inc.

Gough, R. W. (1998). *Character is destiny: The value of personal ethics in everyday life.* Roseville, CA: Prima Publishing.

Harvey, G. (1995). *Writing with sources: A guide for Harvard students. Expository writing program.* The President and Fellows of Harvard University. Retrieved from: http://www.fas.harvard.edu/~expos/sources/.

Haste, H. (1998). Communitarianism and the social construction of morality. *Students Moral Development and Education,* College of Education, University of Illinois. Retrieved from: http://tigger.uic.edu/.

Hill, B. C., Noe, K. S., & King, J. A. (2003). *Literature Circle in Middle School: One Teacher's Journey.* Norwood, MA. Christopher-Gordon Publishing, Inc.

Horgan, J. J. (1989). *Pioneer College: The centennial history of Saint Leo College, Saint Leo Abbey, and Holy Name Priory.* Saint Leo, FL: Saint Leo College Press.

Inlay, L. (2003). Values: The implicit curriculum. *Educational Leadership,* 60(6), 69–71.

Irvin, J. L., Buehl, D. R., & Klemp, R. M. (2003). *Reading and the high school student: Strategies to enhance literacy.* Boston: Allyn and Bacon.

Kagan, S. (1994). *Cooperative learning.* San Juan Capistrano, CA: Kagan Cooperative Learning.

Kaye, D., & Roussos, G. (2000). *Conversation starters as easy as ABC 123: How to start conversations with people who have memory loss.* ABCD Books.

Keats, Jonathon. (2004). Viva Spanglish! Reprinted in *Utne,* No. 122, March–April, 44–47.

Kohlberg, L. (1985). The just community approach to moral education in theory and practice. *Moral Education: Theory and Application.* Lawrence Erlbaum Associates.

Kohlberg, L. (1980). In B. Munsey (Ed.). *Moral development, moral education, and Kohlberg: Basic issues in philosophy, psychology, religion, and education.* Birmingham: Religious Education Press.

Kohlberg, L. (1981). *Essays on moral development. Vol I: The philosophy of moral development.* Retrieved from: The six stages of moral judgment http://www.ccp.uchicago.edu/grad/Joseph_Craig/kohlberg.htm.

Kohn, A. (1997). How not to teach values: A critical look at character education. *Phi Delta Kappa,* February 1997, 429–439.

Krebbs, M. J. (2001). "About my Father's work"—A vehicle for the integration of Catholic values. *Momentum,* 32(1), 14–16.

Knowles, D. D. (1977). *The Benedictines: A digest for moderns.* Saint Leo, FL: The Abbey Press.

Lauber, P. A. (1991). *The New Book of Knowledge.* Danbury, CT: Grolier Inc 7, G.

Leming, J. S. (2001). Historical and ideological perspectives on teaching moral and civic virtue. *International Journal of Social Education,* 16 (1), 62–76.

Lickona, T. (1993). The return of character education. *Educational Leadership,* 11, (51), 6–11.

Light, R. J. (2001). *Making the most of college: Students speak their minds.* Cambridge, MA: Harvard University Press.

Loeller, O., Baumert, J., & Schnabel, K. (2001). Does interest matter? The relationship between academic interest and achievement in mathematics. *Journal for Research in Mathematics Education,* 32 (5), 448–470.

Lundstrom, M. (1999). Character makes a comeback. *Instructor,* 109(3), 25–28.

Mathieson, K., & Bhargava, M. (2003). *Do our students want values programs?* Retrieved from: http://www.colleagevalues.org/seereview.cfm?id+1000.

Mayeaux, A. R. (1993). Towards the fifth century: Dominicans, the other and the 'unavoidable' community. *Providence,* 1 (3), 259–271.

McKeachie, W. J. (1999). Teaching values: Should we? Can we? In W. McKeachie (Ed.), *Teaching tips: Strategies, research, and theory for college and university teachers.* (19th ed.) (pp. 332–344). Boston: Houghton Mifflin.

McKown, H. C. (1935). *Character Education.* New York: McGraw-Hill.

Menslin, J. M. (1999). *Sociology: A down-to-earth approach.* Needham Heights, MA: Allyn & Bacon.

Miles, T. J., & Nance, D. W. (1997). *Mathematics: One of the liberal arts.* Pacific Grove, CA: Brooks/Cole Publishing Company.

Morrison, T. (2001). How can values be taught in the university? *Michigan Quarterly Review, 40*(2), 273–278.

Moustakas, C. (1966). *The authentic teacher: Sensitivity and awareness in the classroom.* Cambridge, MA: Harvard Doyle Publishing.

National Association of College Employers (NACE). (2000). *Job outlook 2000—what employers want.* Retrieved from: http://www.naceweb.org/.

Neuhofer, D., O.S.B. (1999). *In the Benedictine tradition: The origins and early development of two college libraries.* Lanham, MD: University Press of America Inc.

Nieto, S. (2003). *What keeps teachers going?* New York: Teachers College Press.

Noddings, N. (2002). *Educating moral people: A caring alternative to character education.* New York: Teachers College Press.

Nucci, L. (1987). Synthesis of research on moral development. *Educational Leadership, 2,* 82–2.

O'Sullivan, S. (2002). Character education through children's literature. Bloomington, IN: Phi Delta Kappa Educational Foundation.

Palmer, P. (2002). (Personal communications, September 5, 2002). One year later: Exploring the larger questions of having a life after September 11th. An interview with Jon Dalton.

Palmer, P. J. (1998). *The courage to teach: Exploring the inner landscape of a teacher's life.* San Francisco: Jossey-Bass Inc. Publishers.

Partnow, E. (Ed.). (1992). *The new quotable woman.* New York: Facts on File.

Pflaum, W. D. (2004). *The technology fix: The promise and reality of computers in our schools.* Alexandria, VA: Association for Supervision and Curriculum Development.

Principles and practices for promoting character development in college. Retrieved from: www.CollegeValues.org.

Rand, A. (1959). *Atlas shrugged.* Penguin USA.

Rilke, R. M. (1993). *Letters to a young poet.* M. D. Herter Norton (trans.) New York: Norton, 35.

Ritchhart, R. (2002). *Intellectual character: What it is, why it matters, and how to get it.* San Francisco: Jossey-Bass, A Wiley Co.

Rudolph, F. (1990). *The American college and university: A history.* Athens: U of Georgia P.

Sadlier, Right Reverend Abbot Francis, O.S.B., D.D. (1940). *Saint Leo Golden Jubilee 1890–1949: History and illustrations commemorating the founding and activities of the Order of Saint Benedict of Florida at Saint Leo, Florida.* Saint Leo, FL: Abbey Press.

Sax, L. (2003). Citizenship and spirituality among college students: What have we learned and where are we headed? *Journal of College and Character, 2.* Retrieved from: http://www.collegevalues.org.

Schmitz, J. (Ed.) (1992). *Valuing in decision-making: Theory and practice at Alverno College.* Alverno Productions.

Schwartz, A. J. (2000, June 3). It's not too late to teach college students about values. *The Chronicle of Higher Education.*

Scott-Maxwell, F. (1983). *The measure of my days.* New York: Penguin Books.

Scribner's magazine. (1987). Vol. 1, 4, taken from *American memory: The nineteenth century in print.* Retrieved from: http://memory.loc.gov/ammem/ndlpcoop/moahtml/snchome.html.

Shaughnessy, P., O.S.B., Knaebel, B., O.S.B., Galvin, J. P., Ph.D., & Schulte, P. C., D.D. (1956). *The holy rule of our most holy father Saint Benedict.* St. Meinrad, IN: Grail Publications.

Simon, K. G. (2001). *Moral questions in the classroom: How to get kids to think deeply about real life and their schoolwork.* New Haven & London: Yale University Press.

Simon, S., & Kirschenbaum, H. (1972). *Values clarification: A handbook of practical strategies for teachers and students.* Hart Publishing Company.

Simpson, J. B. (1988). *Simpson's Contemporary Quotations: The Most Notable Quotes since 1950.* Boston: Houghton Mifflin.

Stead, J., O.S.B. (1994). *Saint Benedict: A Rule for beginners.* Hyde Park, NY: New City Press.

Stengal, Richard. (2000). *You're Too Kind: A Brief History of Flattery.* New York: Touchstone.

Strange, C. A Benedictine spirituality of engagement and common college classrooms. *Center for the Study of Values in College Student Development, Institute on College Student Values.* Retrieved from: http://www.college/values.org/proceedings.

Strange, C., & Hagan, H. (2000). Reading the signs of the times: A Benedictine pedagogy for building community in higher education. *Proceedings of the Biennial Meeting of the American Benedictine Academy.* St. Meinrad, IN: Archabbey.

Strange, C., & Hagan, H. (1998). Benedictine values and building campus community. *The Cresset: A review of literature, arts, and public affairs,* special issue, 5–11.

Stravinskas, P. M., & Reilly, P. J. (2002). *Newman's idea of a university: The American response.* Newman House Press.

Stringer, D. M., & Cassiday, P.A. (2003). *52 activities for exploring values differences.* Yarmouth, ME: Nicholas Brealey Publishing.

*The Academy, the economy and the liberal arts.* Academe. (1992, July–August, 10–12).

The John Templeton Foundation. (Ed.). (1999). *The Templeton guide: Colleges that encourage character development.* Radnor, PA: Templeton Foundation Press.

The Knight Higher Education Collaborative. (2003). When values matter. *John S. and James L. Knight Foundation in Policy Perspectives,* 1–10.

*The St. Petersburg Times.* Awaiting proof of solved riddle, math hero shies from publicity. (2004, February 8). Section A, 17.

*The St. Petersburg Times.* Today is the last day you can puff away in an Irish pub. (2004, March 28). Section A, 14.

Tompkins, G. E. (1997). *Literacy for the twenty-first century: A balanced approach.* Upper Saddle River, NJ: Merrill/Prentice Hall.

Townsend, (1992). Why kids can't tell right from wrong. *Washington Monthly Magazine.* (Reprinted by permission in *St. Petersburg Times,* Dec. 27, 1992).

Turkle, S. (1984). *The Second Self: Computers and the Human Spirit.* New York: Simon & Shuster.

Wallace, L. P. (1966). *Leo XIII and the rise of socialism.* Duke University Press.

Wanted: Liberal Arts Grads. *Fortune,* May 12, 1997, p. 151.

Weissbourd, R. (2003). Moral teachers, moral students. *Educational Leadership,* 60, 6.

WorldNet (r) 1.6 (1997). Original database from Princeton University. Retrieved from: http://dictionary.com.

Young, R. B. (1997). *No neutral ground: Standing by the values we prize in higher education.* San Francisco: Jossey-Bass.